A Cool Breeze on the Appalachian Trail

A Supported Thru-Hike

TOM GREGG

Copyright© 2018 by Tom Gregg

All rights reserved. This book or any portion thereof may not be reproduced, displayed, or used in any manner whatsoever without the express written permission of the publisher except for the use of brief quotations in a book review.

Cover and Interior Design: Priya Paulraj

ISBN: 978-0-578-42959-5 (hard cover)
ISBN: 978-0-578-43008-9 (e-book)
ISBN: 978-0-578-43757-6 (paperback)

Printed in the United States of America

5 | Things to Remember

Hike your own hike
Pride goeth before a fall
Keep it simple
It is hard work
Have fun

5 | Reasons to Consider a Supported Hike

You can walk farther, faster
Less wear and tear on your body
Focus is on hiking
Sleep and eat where and what you want
It's fun

Contents

Introduction: Supported Hiking .... *xi*
About .... *xvii*
Day 0: Springer Mountain, GA 2
Day 1: What a great First day 4
Day 2: Rain, Rain – I loved it 7
Day 3: Take a guess, Rain 9
Day 4: Goodbye GA Hello NC 11
Day 5: I Met a Girl 15
Day 6: Forrest Gump 18
Day 7: One Week Down 21
Day 8: Happy Memorial Day 23
Day 9: By the Numbers 26
Day 10: Goodbye Smoky Mountains 30
Day 11: She Did It 33
Day 12: Hot Tub on the Trail 35
Day 13: Fear of Heights 38
Day 14: The Scooby Doo Mobile 41
Day 15: Comments? 46
Day 16: Goodbye NC 49

Day 17: Now Streaming 52
Day 18: Where is the bear? 55
Day 19: Bears! Bye TN hi VA 59
Day 20: The Grayson Highlands 62
Day 21: Be careful what you wish for 65
Day 22: 25% of the Trail completed 68
Day 23: Meeting more thru hikers 71
Day 24: Happy Birthday Sara 73
Day 25: Hiked with Poppins 75
Day 26: This is hard 78
Day 27: Dragons Tooth 81
Day 28: Happy Father's Day 84
Day 29: 1/3 of the way 87
Day 30: The day after 90
Day 31: My first rattlesnake 92
Day 32: Cousin Mac visits Cool Breeze 95
Day 33: Trump tweets about Cool Breeze 97
Day 34: Shin Splints 99
Day 35: A visit home 101
Day 36: Back on the Trail 104
Day 37: A visit from Tom 106
Day 38: 1,000 Miles! 109
Day 39: The fastest so far 111
Day 40: I'm in the North 114
Day 41: 1/2 Way! 116
Day 42: A much better day 120
Day 43: Not too bad, yet 123
Day 44: Happy 4th of July 126
Day 45: Ah oui, the rocks 129

Day 46: Slippery Rock...131
Day 47: Not my finest hour 133
Day 48: Rocks be damned 136
Day 49: Great day in NJ 138
Day 50: I met a Scallywag 141
Day 51: Welcome to NY 144
Day 52: Back to Bear Mountain...147
Day 53: Hot and Humid 149
Day 54: 2/3 of the way..152
Day 55: New shoes 155
Day 56: Welcome to Massachusetts 158
Day 57: Audio Books 161
Day 58: Liking MA now 163
Day 59: Into Vermont...165
Day 60: A Tough Mudder 167
Day 61: Vermud...169
Day 62: Harry Potter 172
Day 63: Oh Happy Day..174
Day 64: Near 0 day 176
Day 65: Welcome to NH...178
Day 66: I wore my backpack..180
Day 67: Grandma Smithwood to the rescue............................183
Day 68: Man of Wheel..185
Day 69: Spectacular Views 187
Day 70: A shorter day...189
Day 71: Mt. Washington...191
Day 72: The Wildcats 195
Day 73: Finished the White Mountains 196

Day 74: Maine 199
Day 75: Mahoosuc Notch 201
Day 76: Beat out the rain 203
Day 77: Pushing Through.. 205
Day 78: Weather held out.. 208
Day 79: 2,000 Miles 210
Day 80: My Wife's Birthday... 213
Day 81: Mick the Moose.. 216
Day 82: It ain't over till it's over 218
Day 83: I saw a moose 220
Day 84: We are getting close 222
Day 85: We did it!! Many, many thanks! 224
*Dad's Zombieland additional Rules learned while
hiking the Appalachian Trail — for Caroline* *228*
Postscript: August 2018 .... *232*
Frequently Asked Questions: *241*
Appendix... *249*
Appalachian Trail Statistics *249*
My Appalachian Trail Statistics.. *249*
My Supply / Packing List.. *251*
My Plan *257*
Final Pictures.. *278*

Introduction: Supported Hiking

Our world continues to advance each year in many ways, as do our interests in how and where we recreate. When I was young, there were no smartphones, ultra-light backpacks, GPS apps, or Uber drivers. All the kids in my neighborhood would play together outside all day until our parents called us (with a bell) to come to dinner. This was our summer vacation. Kids today are different, with different interests, wants and needs. I am very different today, as the world appears much smaller to me than when I was a kid. Instead of setting out to dig a hole until I reached China, I can get on a plane and I am in China in fourteen hours. I have lived there twice and traveled there many times. I have walked on the Great Wall and hiked in search of giant pandas in southwest China. In fact, I have had the opportunity to travel to many places around the world. I have gone on a safari in South Africa and hiked in Patagonia, at the southern tip of South America. I have cruised to Alaska and to the Arctic in Norway. I have ridden camels in Egypt and run from the Eifel Tower to Versailles. The opportunities for people to travel are endless today. I hope to get to do it all. Most all of my adventures were supported by someone—some group or some company. Should the experience of hiking the Appalachian Trail (AT) be limited to those who backpack?

Twenty years ago (1998), Bill Bryson published a *New York Times* bestseller (and the most famous book about the Appalachian Trail) about his journey, *A Walk in the Woods*. It was extremely funny and well written.

However, when I read it many years ago, I was reading it as a person who had always wanted to hike the Appalachian Trail, and his journey was not an experience that I wanted to have. I started wondering if hiking the AT was something I really wanted to do, as I did not think that walking through the "Long Green Tunnel" for many months with a heavy backpack sounded all that exciting to me. Over the years, when the thought of me hiking the AT came up, I was assured by my friends who had done it and from reading the many AT books on the market that it did not have to be that way. In fact, everyone's hiking experiences were very different. However, there was really no getting past the backpacking/tent camping aspect of hiking the trail. As I got closer to actually thinking that this hike could come to fruition, I learned of ways to hike the AT that I thought would make me happy, successful, and would be in my comfort zone. I came to use the brilliantly written Bryson book as what *not* to do on the AT. I wanted to do a "supported hike," with a lot of physical, mental and logistical preparation. I wanted to hike long miles each day carrying very little, and taking no rest days. This was the exact opposite of what Bryson did. And, I hoped ultimately to hike the entire Appalachian Trail, which he did not accomplish.

    I truly believe that supported hiking is an excellent way to give more people—people for whom it would not otherwise be possible—the opportunity to experience the wonders and beauty of the Appalachian Trail while protecting it from overcrowding and other associated issues. It is also a way of keeping it from becoming irrelevant with so many choices and changing lifestyles as to how and where one spends their time and money.

    Adventure tourism is experiencing exponential growth around the world. People want to do more than just look at a monument from a bus or lie on a beach somewhere during their precious free time. People want to improve their health on their vacation while still having an incredible, memorable time. For their precious dollar, many people want to do something active. When it comes to the Appalachian Trail, most people believe the only way to experience it is to strap on a heavy backpack, and live on and with whatever you are strong enough to carry with you. The expectation is that you will sleep in a tent. Some people love that, and they often believe the Trail is reserved for them. Many people do not want to do that or cannot do that, but would probably love to experience the AT for more than an afternoon. They are too old, too inexperienced, too scared, too used to their creature comforts or just do not enjoy camping. So, they never really get to experience much of the AT. The other popular way people experience the AT is as a day hiker. This is usually at a highly trafficked area associated with a well-known park or forest. This is how the vast majority of the 3 million people a year who hike on the AT experience it. These areas constitute a very small part of the 2,200 miles of trail from Georgia to Maine. So, the more tourism concentrates at these spots, the more congested and the harder it is to protect those portions of the Trail.

If you knew that you could hike parts the AT for a week, and in the evening stay at a nice hotel, B&B, or "Glamp," eat a nice meal, and even enjoy a spa, would you be more interested? For some people, the answer is no. They want to backpack and camp in the woods in tents or stay at shelters. I am all for that, if that is what you want. For others who would not do it otherwise, the answer is probably yes.

There is a great "hut" system along the AT in New Hampshire run by the Appalachian Mountain Club (AMC). If you are a good hiker, and have the financial means, you can stay in a full service hut each night on the AT while hiking through the White Mountains. These huts in the summer provide dinner and breakfast, a bunk bed and blanket, and some nature programs for entertainment. Everything is eco-friendly and all food is carried in and trash carried out by the young staff. I think it would be so great to have opportunities like this up and down the Trail, not just in New Hampshire. This is actually what Benton MacKaye envisioned when he came up with the idea for the AT in the 1920s.

Many of the communities adjacent to the AT, particularly in the south, would benefit greatly from increased tourism. There are currently forty-six designated AT trail towns. If people would come off the trail in the evenings and stay in lodgings, eat breakfast and dinner in town, and shop in local stores, it would likely provide jobs and other economic benefits to these communities. Hikers would in turn feel more welcome and appreciated in towns. The potential negative impacts of more people getting on and off the AT at lesser known access points include people not adhering to the Leave No Trace rules jeopardizing the natural wilderness that is the AT, not to mention security concerns of hikers mixing with those just walking in to "party" for the evening, or with other nefarious intent.

I am now a Board Member of the Appalachian Trail Conservancy (ATC). The ATC is the guardian of the Appalachian Trail. It is the volunteer-based organization that preserves and manages the entire AT in conjunction with federal, state, and local governments and numerous other volunteer groups. I do not speak for the ATC, but I know our mission is to make the trail safely available so all Americans can see and experience it, not just backpackers. It is also in our mission to protect the Trail and the Trail experience. We have to be innovative and creative, therefore, to meet the needs of present-day tourism.

So, how do we evolve with differing and changing ideas in the hyper-growth adventure tourism market in order to maximize the number of people to safely experience the wonder of the AT? One option is to do nothing and just let the market figure it out. It will slowly evolve and we at the ATC will react. Another option is to promote new and different ways to experience the Trail. Within the Adventure Tourism market is "ecotourism." We can create programs that promote volunteerism on the Trail, programs that promote diversity on the Trail, and programs that promote education on the Trail.

I believe that supported hiking is a relatively new concept in the USA. It has been very popular in Europe for a long time. For example, in the UK, there are many private hiking companies offering long distance group hikes, and companies that will transport your "stuff" each morning to the place you will be at the next night. People have been doing supported hikes (pilgrimages) on the Camino de Santiago in Spain for more than a thousand years.

Supported bike trips in the US are very popular as it easier for the bikers to get to hotels and restaurants in another town every day; and it is easier to drive a van along with them in case they get tired, have a flat, or need supplies. I do get many email advertisements for companies like Backroads and the Wildland Trekking Company for supported hiking trips in the US, so I know it is becoming more popular.

When I go on a vacation, I have to have a cell signal and charged battery for work, family, security, and pleasure. This is not negotiable. How do I charge my phone? Is there a signal? A hiking purist would say you need to leave your phone at home. For some, that is the right lesson for everyone. For others, it is a showstopper. I believe that everyone needs to hike their own hike while protecting the Trail without disturbing the enjoyment of others. Supported hiking is a way to get more people to experience the magnificence of the Appalachian Trail; and getting more people to experience and protect places like the Appalachian Trail is the main reason why the National Trail System Act was established more than fifty years.

There are many versions of supported hikes, but the basic concept is that you are a day hiker for an extended period of time—days, weeks, even months. Usually, there needs to be at least two people involved, but I have seen it done with one person who had a truck and a motorcycle. The hiker would put the motorcycle on his truck and drive to where he would be at the end the day. Then he would drive the truck back to the start and hike to his motorcycle and ride it back to the truck, continuing the process each day. There can be two people with two vehicles or two people with one vehicle, but usually that means people are hiking each day in opposite directions. Warren Doyle, through his Appalachian Trail Institute (ATI), has been offering group van-supported thru-hikes of the AT that he calls "expeditions" once every few years for decades. There are more and more services being offered throughout the Trail where drivers will pick you up from the Trail and take you to town. Of course, there are also guided hike options, both private and group-based, which I believe will be more available in the future.

It is my prediction that in the next ten years self-driving/autonomous cars will be available to meet you at road crossings so you could support your own hike. This book chronicles how I did my supported thru-hike.

When I hiked the AT, I kept a trail journal every day that I uploaded to an Internet website that I developed specifically for the hike. The following are the actual journal entries (with a little editing for spelling and grammar) that I wrote every night and the comments that I got from friends, families, and well-wishers. It is how I hiked my own hike every day. I hope you find it enjoyable. As a postscript, I also wrote about my experience over the next year following my hike. That was quite a supported journey also. I have also tried to answer many of the questions that I was asked when I got back home that I did not answer in my journal. Finally, I have included some statistics from the Trail, my packing list, and my overall plan—and a few final pictures that I thought were fun.

Hope you enjoy this. . . .

ABOUT

Who?

My name is Cool Breeze (AKA Tom Gregg) and I will be fifty-three years old when I start the hike. Thru-hikers usually take on an alias or "trail name" when they hike the Appalachian Trail. Some people choose their own trail name and others have their name given to them by another hiker. I gave myself the trail name of Cool Breeze. I actually thought a lot about what my trail name should be (I think a lot about everything). I am currently the co-owner of the Medium Rare restaurants in the Washington DC area. In the US, our identity is often closely linked to our career—I am a doctor, lawyer, chef, stockbroker. As an entrepreneur, I have had many identities; the latest is as a restaurateur. I thought hard about making Medium Rare my trail name. I have also been lucky enough to live in China a couple of times, and I had a business there and here for ten years (3GI). In China, I was known as Cool Breeze (Liang Feng). I decided I wanted to use this as my trail name, as a cool breeze comes and goes quickly; it is enjoyable when warm and stinks when cold. When I lived in Paris, helping to run the great food manufacturer Cuisine Solutions, I tried to go by Tom-Louie, incorporating my middle name, but it never caught on. For my three months on the trail, I still need to be working (the ultimate telecommute). Medium Rare as my trail name (my business partner Mark wanted me to be Secret Sauce) would have been a good way to remind me of what is allowing me to do this unbelievable journey in the way I am choosing to do it. However, I think I will start out as Cool Breeze (or just Cool for short) but maybe I will change it if Cool Breeze does not catch on or feel right. For now, I am Tom Gregg, the restaurant owner of Medium Rare, and also the thru-hiker Cool Breeze. Oh, the picture of me was not taken on the Appalachian Trail (there are no giant saguaro cactus on the Trail). It was taken on a recent trip to Tucson with my wife to visit my life-long friends, the Darling family.

What?

I am doing a supported thru-hike or more specifically a Supported Endurance Thru-Hike (SETH)—I just made this acronym up—of the Appalachian Trail. What that means is I am going to hike the entire 2,189 miles of the Appalachian Trail from Georgia to Maine, really fast, with some help. In fact, it is my goal to hike the 2,189 miles in ninety days or less. This means that I have to walk almost a marathon distance each day, through the mountains with an average daily elevation gain loss of over 5,000 feet, for ninety consecutive days. See "why" below for my attempt to explain why I would want to do this.

A thru-hike is defined as walking the Appalachian Trail in its entirety, always following the white blazes that mark the Trail. A thru-hiker is someone who is attempting to hike the entire Trail all at once. This is what I am attempting to do. I know I will encounter many people out for the day (day hikers) or some will be out for the weekend or longer; some people will hike the trail a section at a time (section hikers) which is usually a few hundred miles or more. This year, there will likely be more than 5,000 people attempting to thru-hike the trail. The average thru-hike takes between five and seven months to complete. Only around 25 percent complete it. I hope to be one of the 25 percent. (Read "how" to see how I am going about improving my odds to finish.) It takes around 5 million steps to complete. There is, of course, some luck involved, as you could turn an ankle or a knee on any step, or suffer a myriad of other mishaps or happenings that could be the end of the hike—even on the first day.

There are supported and un-supported hikers on the trail. Although it is difficult for someone to truly hike the trail with no support, there are many people that do their best to hike the trail with little or no help from others. They are a subset of un-supported hikers that are called self-supported hikers. They carry all their own gear and food; they always sleep on the trail, they don't hitchhike to towns; they do their own "maildrops" for supplies and food that they pick up themselves at post offices. I applaud them for that. They are hiking their own hike. An un-supported hiker usually means that the hiker carries his or her own gear and supplies. They are backpackers. They often still stay in hotels and hostels when needed, and get assistance from others when offered, etc., but for the most part, they are carrying what they need—and it is heavy. Even an ultra-light backpacker is still carrying fifteen to twenty pounds when you count food and water. It is also time-consuming finding water, shelter, and getting in and out of towns.

My hike is supported. This means that I will not be carrying my own gear for the most part. I will essentially be a day hiker for ninety days or fewer. I will only carry what I need to get me to the next rendezvous point. This will allow me to walk longer and faster with less wear and tear on my body. In my case, I have a support person, who I will call my Pit Crew Chief—my friend Michael (pronounced Mick-eye-el) from Germany. We have a rented sleeper van that my Pit Crew Chief will drive while supporting me. So, I will have access to plenty of food and drink and a place to sleep (car camping) at road crossings. This will also give me a mobile office so I can work in the evenings. There are over five hundred road crossings on the AT. By the way, Michael is a much more accomplished hiker and adventure traveler than I, having twice hiked through the Australian Outback. I am sure I will be talking about him a lot in daily journal entries. I am going to try to get him to adopt the trail name Mick Dundee (Just call him Mick).

Most thru-hikers take their time backpacking the Trail and they enjoy the whole experience of being in nature day and night, off the grid, relying only on what they can carry; and they usually hike only as far as they want each day. This is not for me. In fact, I do not know if I could mentally or physically do it that way. I respect those who can. I also really do enjoy and respect nature and the trail as I will be walking it for eight to twelve hours a day. However, I have carried a large pack in the past; I have slept in tents; I have searched for water (I have never hitchhiked), and I do not enjoy these activities. At age fifty-three, what I enjoy is to walk as long and as far as I can each day. And, as I only have a short window because I have to continue to work during the hike, and I have a wife and kids at home, a longer, unsupported hike would be impossible for me right now. I think this is going to be a very popular way of hiking in the future when people realize it can be done. In an endurance hike, the goal is still to have fun and make new friends, but also to finish as quickly as possible. Although the Appalachian Trail Conservancy (ATC) does not keep speed records, the record on Fastest Known Times for a supported hike of the AT is around forty-five days (half the time of what I am trying to do). I am not trying to break a record, but knowing those times help me believe that I could possibly do this. I know there will be "haters" who say that I should not be hiking the trail "supported" and it's either unsupported or it is cheating. I believe everyone should hike their own hike based on their own particular circumstances, goals, and reasons for doing it. The common thread is that every successful thru-hiker has to hike the entire Appalachian Trail following the white blazes the entire way. I will try to do that.

Where?

The Appalachian Trail (AT) is the longest hiking-only footpath in the world, ranging between Georgia and Maine. It is 2,190 miles long. It traverses 14 states with over 464,500 feet of elevation gain/loss. The idea of the Appalachian Trail came about in 1921. The trail itself was completed in 1937 after more than a decade of work, although improvements and changes continue. It is maintained by thirty-one volunteer Trail clubs and multiple partnerships and managed by the National Park Service, United States Forest Service and the Appalachian Trail Conservancy (ATC). Over 3 million people walk on the trail each year.

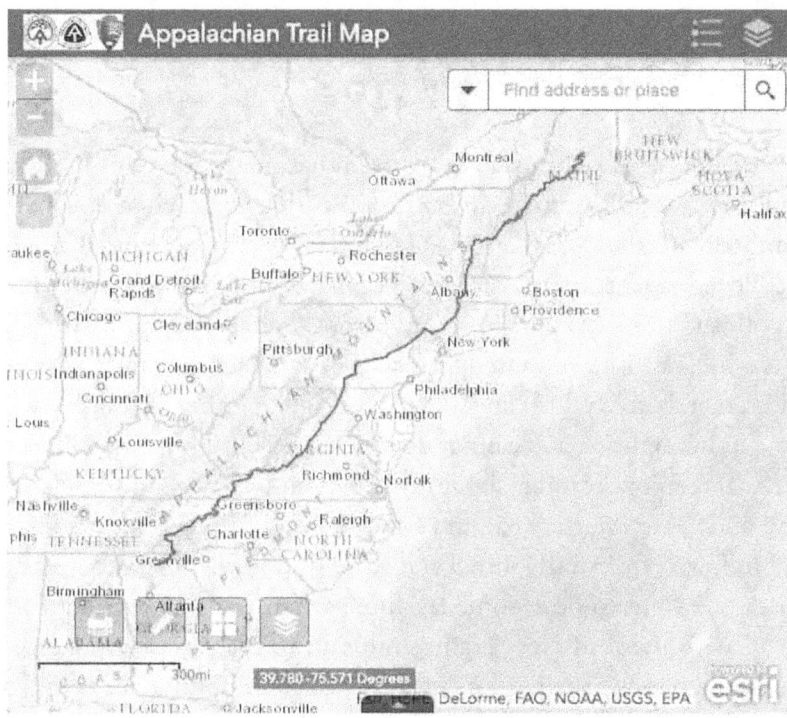

When?

I plan to start the hike at Springer Mountain Georgia on May 22, 2017. I hope to complete it around August 22, 2017 at Mt. Katahdin in Baxter State Park in Maine. A lot of thought went into this time frame. Most thru-hikers going northbound start in March and April (although you can start anytime). So, when I start there will be fewer thru-hikers around me. Most importantly for me, the weather will be warmer as I do not like the cold. As most people are taking five to seven months to hike the trail, at my expected pace I will start to catch up to more and more fellow thru hikers after around thirty days and then I should see a lot of thru-hikers all the way until the finish. With this schedule, it will hopefully still be warm in Maine at Mt. Katahdin at the finish. It is also in the summer when my kids are out of school, so hopefully I might get a visit or two from the family along the Trail.

Why?

People hike the AT for many reasons and at many stages of life. Some people are recently retired and are doing this to re-charge; some are recently divorced or lost their job and do this to get away from it all; some are college students or recent grads hoping to find themselves. I am not doing this (I think) for any of those reasons. I am very happy with where I am in life, but I have wanted to hike the Appalachian Trail as long as I could remember. My Dad always talked about wanting to do it. My Dad is now in his eighties, and cannot do it with me, but I hope he follows my journal and enjoys reading about my experiences. My good friends Don't Mind and Don't Matter (Kit and Lisa) decided to hike the trail in 2004 and I followed their trail journal and successful thru-hike every week and it made me want to do it someday, more and more. My wife and I even met up with them in New Hampshire during their hike and we got to pick them up out of the rain. As my physical conditioning has gotten better and better over the last thirteen years, and I have done some successful long-distance hikes, I decided I thought I could do this. I then learned that there were alternative ways to hike it, and being able to do it my own way made me want to do it even more. I am so lucky and blessed to right now be able to try this hike and be physically, mentally and financially able, and to have the support of my family and business partners. Who knows if I could still do this next year? In the end, I am interested in the experience of doing something, while I can, that I have always wanted to do, and to do it in a way I can really enjoy, and that will be a huge accomplishment for me. I may not succeed, but I think I can do this.

How?

Planning: I am all about planning, as strategy is one of my biggest strengths. I like to plan and then execute that plan. However, there is so much of this hike I cannot plan for and must adapt along the way (not my biggest strength), so I am planning every detail I can and preparing myself mentally to roll with the punches. For example, as I am doing a supported hike, I have to plan for all the rendezvous points. As I am still working, I have to plan on how to do my work and communicate it back and forth. I also need to plan out gear, food and drink, mileage, this journal, communications, finances—the list goes on and on. It does not sound too Zen as I am writing this, but hopefully with all the planning, I can then enjoy the walk and be in the moment most of the time; and then I can find a level of patience (my biggest weakness) when things don't go right.

Physical Training: For the way I plan to hike this, as an endurance hike, physical training and preparation are very important. I will not be anywhere near totally trail-ready at the start (I will have to build up as I go along) as I do not have the time to get used to the daily pounding of eight to twelve hours of walking. Most of the record holders are ultra / trail runners. I am not. However, I have been training specifically for this hike for one year. I try to train six to seven days a week. Last summer I went for three months without a rest day to see how my body held up. I run around forty miles a week, training for ten-mile races. I have been running somewhat competitively now for around thirteen years. I also hike fifteen to twenty miles on average one day each week and try to do strength and core training four to five days a week. It is important I start at the right weight and then maintain it as best as I can as I hike. The goal is to carry as little weight as possible, including not only my pack and clothing, but also my body weight (muscles weight is good). I want to be around 150 pounds, plus or minus five pounds, when I start.

Mental Training: I have probably read more than twenty books about the AT, read scores of trail journals, and talked to people who have done it. Last summer, I attended Warren Doyle's Appalachian Trail Institute (ATI) for a week. It is there I learned that it is not only possible to do a supported hike, but it was the right thing for me. Warren has hiked the entire AT around eighteen times (record). He was once the record holder for fastest time. There is no one who knows more about the Trail than Warren. At the ATI, I learned that the hike is mostly mental. If it rains thirty days in a row, will that stop you? Can you walk through all the pain you are going to feel? I have been running outside almost every day for years and I do it rain, snow, ice, wind, freezing temperatures and heat. I think that will help me a lot as Mother Nature is so unpredictable. At a cold, rainy three-day practice hike on the AT with Warren's group in the fall, I told him that I was thinking of trying to do a one hundred-day endurance thru-hike. He thought I could do it in fewer than ninety days. This has been my goal and mental mindset since.

Experience: I am not doing this having never done any long distance hiking before, so I have a pretty good idea what I am getting into, although the AT is much, much bigger than anything I have ever attempted. I did my first real hike by doing a five-day forty-mile backpacking trip through the backcountry of Yellowstone with my family around six years ago. I really enjoyed the hiking, but not carrying the heavy pack or the tent camping. Two years later, we did a hundred-mile hike on the Cotswold Way in England. This was a great experience. We stayed in B&Bs at night and ate (and drank) at pubs and had our luggage moved each morning by a service to our next location. After that, two years ago, my daughter and I hiked the five hundred mile Camino de Santiago in Spain in twenty-eight days, averaging around nineteen miles a day. This was one of the best experiences ever for me. I recommend it to everyone. We carried light packs and stayed in pilgrim hostels and made so many great friends—including my pit crew chief, Michael from Germany, who is supporting me on the AT. I have also done some training hikes on the AT as well as some recent mountain hikes in the Adirondacks. I cannot wait to get started!

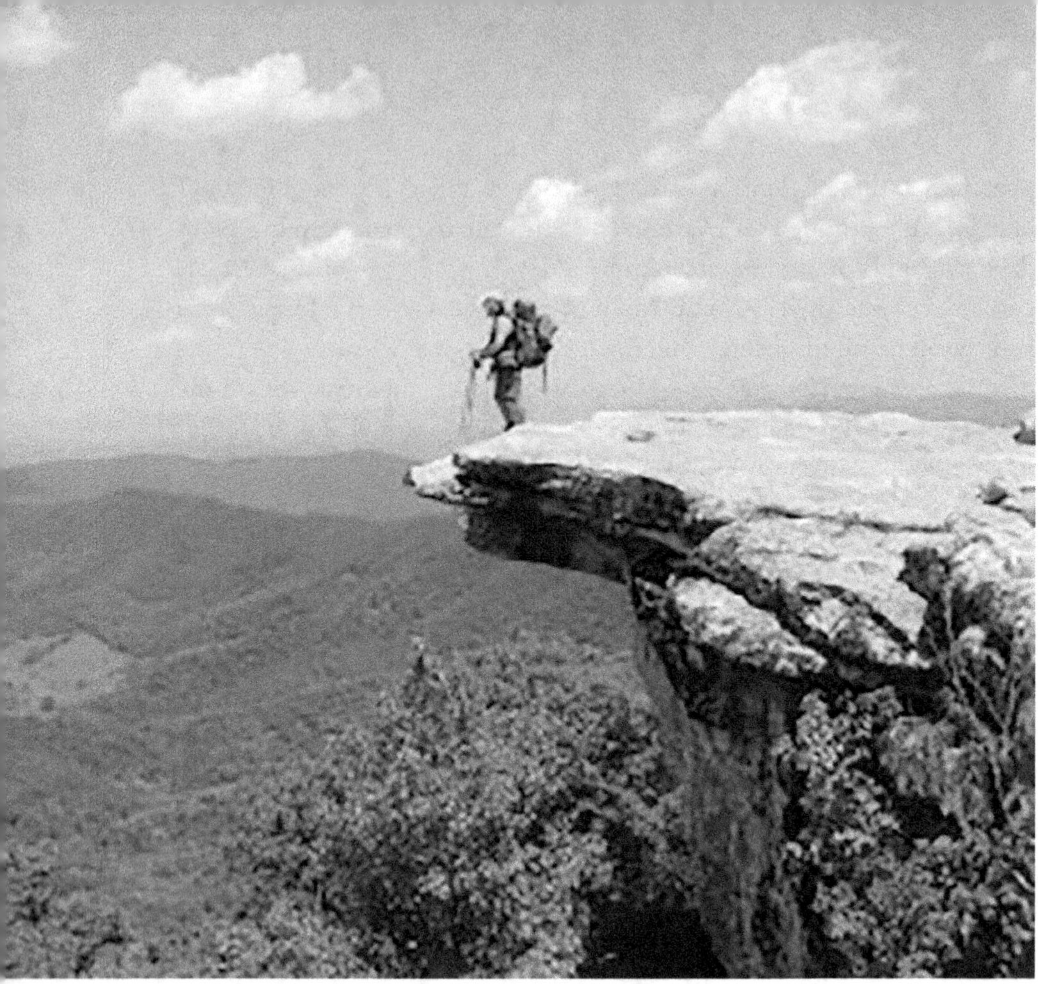

Day 0: Springer Mountain, GA

04/07/2017

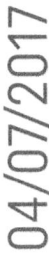

Miles Hiked: 0

Total Miles: 0

Banked Miles: 0

I am planning, training, worrying, and working ahead of my May 22 start. I look forward to updating you on my progress every day. The first post will be May 23, updating you on what happened the previous day. Thanks to Brian Doochin for creating this awesome website for me. Finally, when I get to McAfee Knob around day 26 (see picture above – it is not me), I will never stand anywhere that close to the edge.

6 Comments

bdoochin

   Hey Tom! Good luck out on the trail!

Linda M

   So excited for you. Enjoy!

Ellen S

   We see you on the map —Safe Journey Tom

Jon

   Tom-I'm ready to follow you the whole way and provide encouragement. A few tips to consider—

   *don't drink any brown water

   *be wary of locals in the woods with no teeth that tell you that you "got a pretty mouth"

   *When you are exhausted, wet, cold, bug bitten, scraped up, and sore beyond belief—just know…it can get worse.. and most likely will…

   *Don't forget June 21st is National Nude Hiking Day—do your part!

   Jon

Matt

   Go Tom! Best of luck for the next 89 days!

   Matt

Maggie G

   Jia You Tom !

Day 1: What a great First day

05/23/2017

Miles Hiked: 21.1

Total Miles: 21.1

Banked Miles: -3.2

It was a great first day. My wife, Mick, and Don't Mind and Don't Matter (Kit and Lisa) hiked with me the one mile from the parking lot to the start of the Appalachian Trail (AT) atop Springer Mountain in Georgia. After some pictures, I officially started my hike at 10:15 a.m. on May 22, 2017. We hiked the mile back down and I said goodbye to my wife and she headed home. It was so great having her at the start. Kit and Lisa hiked the entire AT in 2004 and although I have always wanted to hike the Trail, as my father always talked about it, Kit and Lisa inspired me to really do it after I followed their hike. Kit was a leader of my tech company 3GI back in the 1990s. It was so awesome that they would come down and hike the beginning with me. For the first eight miles today, they recounted a lot of stories and gave me a lot of pointers. Then, we said our goodbyes, and I went on another thirteen miles. It was a beautiful day. The plants were in full bloom, the views were spectacular, and the Trail was well maintained. However, at 3:45 it began to rain—big rain, flash flood-type rain. I decided not to put on my rain jacket as I thought I would be too hot. I got out my ball cap and covered my Osprey Talon waist pack with the clear plastic garment bag given to me by Crest Cleaners (best in DC, MD, and VA) and kept walking. After the initial shock of torrential rain, I felt great. It was like cooling off in the ocean on a really hot day. I said to myself, "If you are crazy enough to think this is fun, you might actually be able to do this." Mick met me with around three miles to go and we walked together to our ending destination. His legs were fresher and it was hard to keep up with him at the end, but I liked being pushed. It was a relatively easy hiking day for me. I think the elevation gain/loss was only around 3,000 feet when my average is going to be 5,000 across the course of the Trail. However, I am feeling pretty tired as I write this. I am going to do relatively light miles the next two days and then the daily mileage should increase. Overall, it is hard to describe what a great day it was. I know they are all not going to be like this, but I am going to enjoy it when they are. Cheers to everyone at Medium Rare and thanks for helping make this possible for me.

4 Comments

Adam
> Sounds like a great first day, Tom! Way to go!

Beatrix T
> Way to go Tom, thanks for your first post. Rooting for you from the sidelines! The Takenakas

Valerie
> Yay, you're off to a good start!!

Jeff J
> Tom, Congrats on crossing the starting line! I look forward to following your journey.

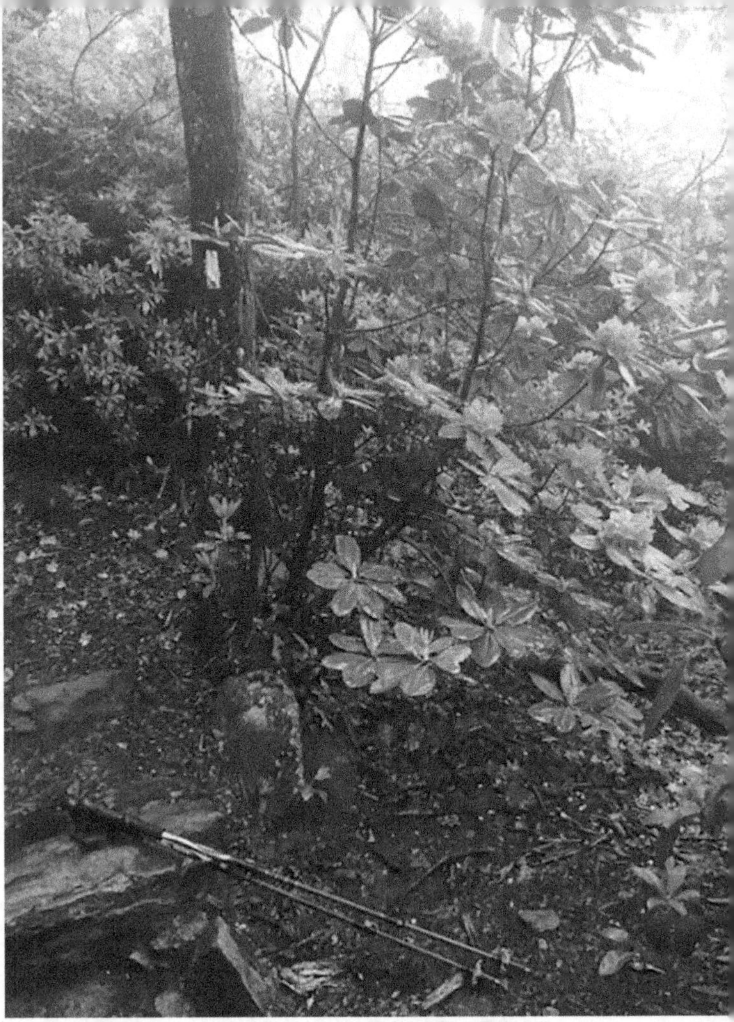

Do you see the white blaze?

Day 2: Rain, Rain – I loved it

Miles Hiked: 17.5

Total Miles: 38.6

Banked Miles: -10

05/24/2017

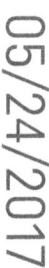

I hiked up and down a bunch of mountains today, the highest being Blood Mountain. It was again not too hard for me, but I think that will change soon. We came to a place around noon today where Kit and Lisa (Don't Mind and Don't Matter) left their car a few days earlier and they planned to hike to it on Thursday. However, it was not there. We think it was towed. I think they will Mind when they arrive as it will Matter. We will stand by to help them as Kit insisted on being out of communications to enjoy the Trail, so we cannot get ahold of him now.

This evening, we ran across a town in Georgia called Helen. It had been suffering the fate of so many small towns in America, so they decided to make it into a German Bavarian-themed town. We had to go there and check it out and get Mick a taste of home. It seemed so out of place in Appalachian Georgia, but everyone was so nice and I thought it was so creative of them to re-invent themselves I was happy to give them our dinner business. I had some great German wurst.

Finally, I want to say congratulations again to Dan and Jacquie on their new marriage. My wife and I went to their beautiful wedding outside Orlando on Saturday before driving to Georgia. Dan is my wife's cousin and he and his new bride are both young medical doctors. He lived with us for a short and extremely fun time during a rotation in DC. Many of my wife's family members are very accomplished hikers and they are all great to see and talk to, so my last days before the hike were really nice.

One Comment

Ellen S
   Many smiles in this post—thanks, Tom—keep going

Mick at BBQ World.

Day 3: Take a guess, Rain

Miles Hiked: 31
Total Miles: 69.6
Banked Miles: -3.4

05/25/2017

Sorry for the late post—I had no Internet last night. OK, Day 3 started as Day 2 ended (and Day 1)—with more rain. The big internal debate in the morning was, "rain jacket or no?" I had yet to pull out the jacket because I will get so hot and sweaty on the climbs wearing it. It was raining hard and it was also quite chilly so I decided on the jacket. You know what they say—"chili today, hot tamale." This is one of my three jokes that I tell again and again. It drives my kids crazy. So, I am out on the Trail for two hours in the rain feeling good about my choice when I encountered the first person. He was wearing only a tee shirt and shorts. I felt for some reason that I had to explain myself to him, "I usually don't wear a jacket either." Because the jacket kept me very warm and dry, a "cool breeze" was good today. Some days cool breeze is good—some days not so good.

Today was going to be my last warm-up day before I started doing bigger miles. However, I was done with nineteen miles at 1:30 pm and we were at the top of a mountain on a really bad, winding road that was miles from anywhere. The next potential rendezvous point was twelve miles farther. I was feeling really good, so I decided to go for it. If my legs hurt tomorrow, I only have to do sixteen miles to be back on plan. My other choice is twenty-nine miles and then I am way ahead and I would have to re-work my plan. Stay tuned. There were many steep climbs today but the Trail was mainly soft dirt, making it pretty easy both up and down. I only saw four hikers the entire day. I was thinking that was odd, but I have no real basis of comparison as I have only been on the Trail three days.

I finished at 6 p.m. at Dick's Creek Gap and we drove into the town of Hiawassee, Georgia for some southern BBQ. It is famous for being the town where the movie *Deliverance* was filmed. I bought Mick a tee-shirt. When you look at the picture of Mick at the BBQ restaurant, zoom in on the man behind him. We are going to sleep with the van alarm on tonight.

I am having so much fun!

One Comment

Kevin
  Thirty-one miles in one day?? You da man! Go, Tom. Go.

Selfie at GA/NC Border

Day 4: Goodbye GA Hello NC

Miles Hiked: 28.9
Total Miles: 98.5
Banked Miles: 1.2

05/25/2017

I awoke to the sound of rain. It was to be a jacket day: both rainy and chilly (insert my joke here). I left at 7 a.m. and arrived at the NC border (no wall there yet) at 10 a.m. This means I completed the Georgia portion of the Trail in almost exactly three days (I started at 10:15 a.m. on Monday). So, Georgia: check mark. We really enjoyed Georgia. The Trail was well maintained and not too difficult. The people we met were "all" really nice.

The most interesting was Bob who runs the hostel/outfitter next to Dick's Creek Gap. Mick and I went there to take a shower. It was my first one. I know you are thinking—gross, but I have been in the pouring rain every day so I have been taking natural showers, right? Anyway, Dick was a character who liked to talk. I quickly learned that he was a contestant on *Naked and Afraid*. I have had questions from watching the show that I always wanted to ask someone who was on it. I got to ask. . . . His is also one of the iconic stops where people arrive with fifty to sixty pound packs, already ready to call it quits in their first weeks. He weighs their packs and then starts removing everything and putting most of it in a box to mail home. They leave the hostel with twenty-five to thirty pounds in their pack, much happier. Every single book on the AT talks about this. It is amazing how many people still carry too much at the beginning and get discouraged. Bob reminded me that on a difficulty scale of one to ten (ten being New Hampshire), Georgia is a four. North Carolina is more like an eight, so I know harder times are on their way for me.

I decided to do the twenty-nine miles today. There was only one road crossing sixteen miles in and Mick was going to meet me there. I only saw one person during the entire trek. Over 3 million people utilize the AT each year and yet here there's only one person besides me. Did I not get the memo? Anyway, it started with put on the jacket, take off the jacket, put on the jacket ("wax on, wax off"). It kept getting colder and windier so the jacket stayed on. Then it was put on the hood, take off the hood. The Trail was a little harder than the previous day due to rocks, but I got through the sixteen miles. But then, no Mick and no van. This was our first logistics malfunction. We had both gotten confused because of the additional miles on Day 3 and Mick had driven to the twenty-ninth mile and started walking in. This meant I had to go thirteen more miles, with no break. Yesterday, we rendezvoused twice. During our 30-minute meeting time I drink a lot, resupply food and drink, change my wet socks and apply Hiking Goo to my feet (yes, a real product to prevent blisters) and rotate my shoes. Oh, and I rest a bit. I always bring extra food and drink, so I was OK there for another four hours, but my feet don't like being wet for nine or ten hours. I am a little tired now; resting the feet; developing a new plan to ensure this doesn't happen again; and still having a great time on top of a mountain in North Carolina. P.S., Kit's car was not towed—false alarm.

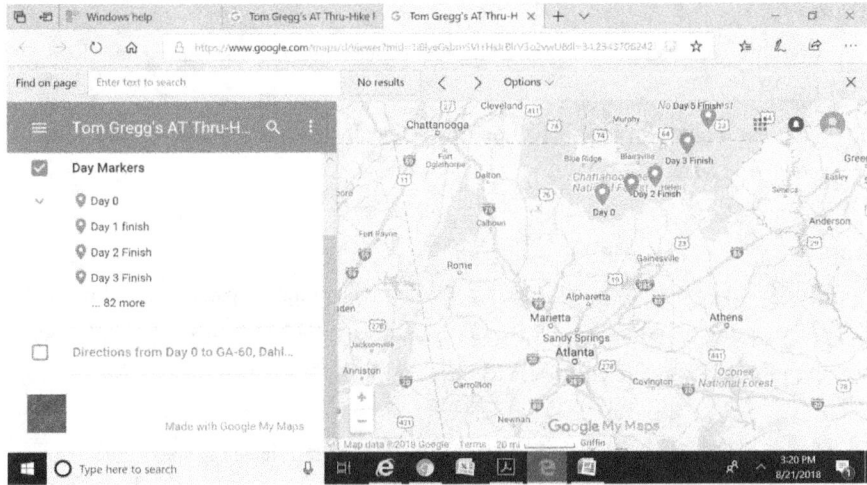

A little Perspective of where I started in Georgia and where I am right now in North Carolina

12 Comments

Kathy

Good Luck, Tom. Cheering you on!

Charles and Kathy

Steve H

Sounds wet, but fun. The solitude of wilderness is amazing . . . even when you are on a trail that sees so much traffic. After some crazy blisters my last marathon, I've been using RunGoo, so I like where you're going with the HikeGoo. It is great stuff.

Keep up the entertaining posts and enjoy the amazing scenery!

Valerie

Keep up the great work! Hope you get some sunshine soon. Thanks for joining us for Dan and Jacquie's wedding! We had fun, and loved seeing you and the family!

Uncle Kevin

impressive back to back distances! Glad to see you're carrying the rain gear.

Ellen S

Tom, we are back at HL, and now can devote more time to commenting. It will be a rainy Memorial Day here so we will be thinking of you more often—keep trekking!!! Hoping for dry days soon.

Karen O

Awesome Tom. What a journey. Can't wait to see what unfolds. All my best. KO

Bobby M

Cool Breeze, I am vicarously (sp) on this hike with you—please keep up the posts. You are the Man...

Bobby

Sara

CONGRATS on finishing Georgia, Dad!! love you and miss you a ton. It sounds like you're getting some authentic AT trail experiences, and I love hearing the stories. Keep up the good work and keep those feet dry! <3

Al

Having a toast to you on the deck. Be careful and watch those big toes.

Al and Melissa

Dirty

Love reading your posts, Tommy! I'd like to know what you asked Bob.... You can share the next time you are in AZ.

Mark T

Hey Tom... sorry its been so wet. Hoping some nicer weather ahead. Sounds like you are doing great and it sounds pretty daunting. Keep it up!!!

Beatrix T

What were those questions to the *naked and afraid* contestant? Addicted to that show. Cheering you on from afar.

Elisabeth and I: One hundred done and one hundred to go

Day 5: I Met a Girl

Miles Hiked: 25.9

Total Miles: 124.4

Banked Miles: 2.8

05/27/2017

Oh what a beautiful morning. Oh what a beautiful day. I've got a beautiful feeling. Everything's going my way (Substitute North Carolina for Oklahoma). I got a little bit of a late start at 7:20 a.m. and NO RAIN, so I wore my lightest running jacket as we were at around 4,500 feet and it was a little chilly (fill-in joke here). The jacket lasted just ten minutes as I was climbing straight up Albert Mountain. I had to put my hands down for the first time, twice, to pull myself up a couple rocks (Thanks to my younger daughter for her climbing training.). I got up to the top in around forty minutes. What a view! I took a picture and had my Chevy Chase / Griswold at the Grand Canyon in the *National Lampoon Vacation* movie moment; said OK to myself and moved on.

I hiked for a couple hours, mainly downhill, and I had again seen nobody. Then, I went around a corner and there she was. She shouted, "Tom!" It was my niece Elisabeth. What are the odds of that? My business partner Mark would say, "Bam, time to play the lottery" (actually his sister works for the DC lottery so he knows about that stuff). Elisabeth was hiking southbound. She has only one hundred miles left to complete the entire Trail. As I had just finished one hundred miles, she was at almost 2,100 miles completed. She had taken a "gap year" before starting college to hike the Trail, which I find interesting as everything here is called *Something*-Gap (between mountains). This is quite an accomplishment for her, but just as much for her parents. I know how much they struggled with letting their nineteen-year-old daughter do this. Then, they worried every day about her ("Share my Location" on the iPhone is great). I think someone should buy her mom an "I survived my daughter's AT thru-hike" tee-shirt on Custom Ink (shameless promotion for my friend Marc's company). In fact, at Custom Ink it is so easy to create a tee-shirt, I can do it myself right from the trail. What is your shirt size Cathy?

Fact checker: I had seen a few people that morning; I knew Elisabeth was going to be there; and she didn't shout "Tom!" I am better than most politicians. She was standing in a campsite with her friend Daniel and Mick when I arrived. Daniel and Elisabeth then proceeded to make us perfect poached eggs with Guacamole and hot sauce on hot dog rolls. The only eggs comparable to them are the perfect sous vide poached eggs served with steak and fries for brunch at Medium Rare. The only potentially better ones would be cooked sous vide by the brilliant chefs at Cuisine Solutions. Have you tried the egg bites at Starbucks made by Cuisine Solutions? I don't drink coffee, but I'll go for the eggs (How's that, Stanislas?). Anyway, I told her how proud I was of her—we had attended the Appalachian Trail Institute together and I got to hike with her a few times in VA on her southbound thru-hike. After breakfast and a few pictures, off we went in opposite directions.

The rest of day was gradual three or four mile climbs and then descents of the same distance until it equaled twenty-six miles. There was so much beautiful, panoramic scenery. I could see it all today because of the great weather and the wildfires last summer that burned a lot of the cover. I almost got sick of it (no not really). Cool Breeze felt really good today in the warm and sunny mountains of North Carolina.

3 Comments

Ellen S

    Tom, your journal is terrific. Wonderful observation of 100m to go, 100m done. Thanks for your detail, your humor [which I get] and also your sincere tribute to many who have given you pause, credit and also moral support. Best . . . as you continue.

Jack Jr.

    Tom,

    Great to read about you on your journey. The pictures are wonderful.

    I loved this entry with you meeting Elizabeth as her AT ends and yours begins. What a rare, umm . . . medium rare, treat.

    Good   luck,

    Jack Jr, Lisa and Owen

Kate D

    Hi Tom! I'm finally catching up on your blog, and this one makes me SMILE. How cool that you and Elizabeth crossed paths on the trail. You two will have some great stories to share!

Fire damage the first 13 miles

Day 6: Forrest Gump

05/28/2017

Miles Hiked: 26.3

Total Miles: 150.7

Banked Miles: 4.8

OK, today was by far my toughest day. I was out at 7 a.m. with nice weather. There was a 40 percent chance of rain, but it did not happen. The day was broken into two parts: thirteen miles in the morning and thirteen miles in the afternoon, Mick was to meet me after the first half-marathon at the Nantahala River in NC. The area around the trail in the morning was completely burned from the fire last summer—the entire way. Although it made for great views, like in the fall when the leaves have fallen, there was also a lot of trail erosion, making it a little precarious for me both visually and physically. Overall, it was not hard this morning, and I arrived to find the river was a river rafting spot complete with stores and restaurants, and I got a bacon cheeseburger and a Diet Coke. I also got fries (did not compare with Medium Rare). I left very satisfied and started the second half-marathon. This was much, much harder. I walked seven miles continuously uphill on a mountain called Sassafras (love the name). It went from 1,800 feet to 5,200 feet and then the next six miles were up and down. My legs were shot at around Mile 20 and I slowly limped the last six miles with the help of Mick. However, in the words of the Argentine professional soccer player from *The Bachelor*, "It's OK." (My sweet sister Jenn will get the reference because we watched the TV show *The Bachelor* together as bonding time, really). I think I just need an Advil or two (adult vitamins). Anyway, tomorrow will be a shorter day, so hopefully I will have the afternoon to work on Medium Rare business.

Now, down to the real business of the day: There has been much chatter on other media today by some of my closest friends that I should change my trail name to Forrest Gump. How did I know that was coming? To be clear, the only comparisons to me and this hike to Forrest Gump are: It is my all-time favorite move; his reason for running back and forth across the US, "I just felt like running"; I am a really good ping-pong player and lived in China; I do think life is like a box of chocolate; and we both married beautiful women. Other than that, there is no comparison. Well, if my mom had seen the movie, she would probably say about this hike, "stupid is as stupid does." I was not an All-American football player, nor a war hero, nor did I teach Elvis to dance. It would also be very hard to change my Trail name. I met section hikers Bill and

Debbie on the Trail today and they were the first people I told I was Cool Breeze, so how can I change it now? Also, I would have to change my website and website address, and get new business cards (I don't really have Cool Breeze business cards—yet). I actually think it was a little insulting. They could have thought something more like, James Bond. My dad's name is James and I have a bond portfolio? I think I will keep Cool Breeze for now as the name felt really good as I was hiking today.

One Comment

Jeff M

Tom

I just read your first six days. I am so impressed with what you are doing. It really is inspirational. I might meet you at Bear Mountain on the Hudson just north of Manhattan. It is right off of the Trail. Let me know which day you think you might be in that area. Good luck!!

Jeff

Day 7: One Week Down

Miles Hiked: 16
Total Miles: 166.7
Banked Miles: -3.5

05/29/2017

I am now sitting with Mick at Fontana Dam—the beginning of the Great Smoky Mountain National Park. It was a short day because tomorrow and the next day will be hard. "This period of relative inactivity is about to come to an end," says my good friend Tom Barr. He would usually say this to our software programmers at my old company 3GI when a big deliverable to the Government was about to be due. There are no road crossings for thirty-three miles and I will climb to the highest point on the AT, 6,667 feet, at Clingmans Dome. We are at 1,800 feet now. It is higher than Mt. Washington in New Hampshire. The next day will be even longer, with no meet-ups until the end.

Late last night was a severe thunderstorm. I was very happy to be safe and cozy in the Scooby Doo-Mobile. I felt so sorry for everyone tent camping, as it was really bad. The morning started again with rain. All the hikers I spoke to yesterday were really worried about Jacobs Ladder. So, of course, I was worried. In the end, it was easy with fresh legs and my little pack. I was up to the top in forty minutes and moving on with the sun now shining. At the end of the day, it would have been hard. I moved a lot of debris from the trail today. Usually, I just catch all the spider webs in my mouth for all the later-rising hikers. Gotta get some rest.

3 Comments

Graceful
> This is a remarkable journey of patient endurance and fulfilled dreams. How glad I am to experience it from dry confines! Tommy, seriously, hope this time is opening up beauty and reflection. Thanks for inviting me along. Graceful

Jon
> So far so good Tom—looking forward to hearing about Clingmans Dome! Had no idea it was that high in altitude. Enjoy it!!
> Jon

Andre
> Feels like Patagonia! Proud of you Bro. Consider attaching a cause and raising some dough. Go Strong and stay like those cool ocean breezes!

Tom and Mick on Clingmans Dome Tower

Day 8: Happy Memorial Day

Miles Hiked: 32.7
Total Miles: 199.4
Banked Miles: 4.9

05/30/2017

Today I hiked for twelve hours from Fontana Dam to Clingmans Dome in the Smoky Mountains. Altogether today, I climbed around 11,000 feet and descended about 6,000 feet. Mick drove the van two hours to Clingmans Dome then hiked in ten miles to meet me. He brought in supplies (food and drink) to get me through the hike. OK, no haters here. I started the morning with my usual can of Diet Mountain Dew and topped it off with around twelve ounces of PowerAde Zero. I ate two Nutri-Grain bars. I was out the door as soon as the sun came up at 6:15 a.m. I packed two twenty-ounce water bottles of half- PowerAde Zero half-water and one twenty-ounce PowerAde Zero. I also packed two ham and cheese sandwiches as well as three Nature Valley bars. When I met Mick at Mile 23, he brought me two thirty-two-ounce PowerAde Zeros (I immediately drank one), a bag of trail mix (love the M&Ms / hate the raisins), and two more ham and cheese sandwiches (as well as a third pair of socks). This got me to the finish line. We are both tired. We are now on the Tennessee / NC border. The trail follows the TN/NC border until around Damascus, Va. The weather held out until a mile from the top. Mother Nature felt we needed to be cooled down for the final ascent. I am not sure if either of us will be up for the thirty-eight miles tomorrow. We are discussing. It could be a short day as it is either eight miles or thirty-eight miles because of the lack of road crossings in the Park.

I cannot explain how lucky and grateful I feel every day getting to do this and how each mile is a fun and a new experience. On this Memorial Day holiday, I thought about my wife and my grandparents and our close relatives no longer with us. I thought about those who lost their lives in service of our country. I also thought a lot about our good friend Gelacio, one of our first and best Medium Rare employees. He has been fighting cancer this year at just age twenty-two. He stills comes to work whenever he is up to it. What I am doing is so much easier than what he is going through—I mostly have control, except for Mother Nature. Also, I think of our friend Joan Wabschall, who has been battling breast cancer for years now, and all the Starlight Children's Foundation families who have to battle illness every day. Nothing I do on this hike, no matter how many miles I do each day, can compare to that. This week, Mick and I got to pay it forward a little helping a father and a daughter who had injured her foot get back to family. We also gave Trail magic (apples, bananas and chocolate) to one-year cancer survivor, thru-hiker Super Dave, and his thru-hiker companions. Hopefully, there will be more opportunities to pay it forward on this trip.

4 Comments

Catherine L

Wow! Doing all if that elevation in one day is incredible. Hoping you'll sleep well tonight! There's some good food coming up in Hot Springs, I think. Glad you've had some better weather.

Sid B

Super inspiring, Tom! Wishing you good weather, beautiful views, and plenty of time for introspection and joy!

Graceful

Tommy, I am exceedingly proud of you and admire you my childhood friend of MANY years! Who knew that the training around the track at SMU would lead to such an endeavor. Seriously, it is a beautiful image, you rustling and chugging and gliding through the Appalachian trail, meeting strangers and remembering loved ones and brave souls. Peter will join your blog. I'll be keeping up from Hong Kong, as we head out tonight from NJ. Peace friend,

Graceful

Alexandra D

Great pics! Keep it up. You rescue people everywhere. You're sorely missed.

A little more American culture for Mick.

Day 9: By the Numbers

05/31/2017

Miles Hiked: 7.7

Total Miles: 207.1

Banked Miles: -11.7

My friend John Corso is one of the smartest and best businessmen I know. He is president of Coastal Produce. It is probably now the biggest (and definitely the best) produce supplier on the east coast. I tell you this because I think he would not find the value of his time reading my whole blog post because of the "fluff" I put in it (like this). I am sure that he scans the numbers now and then to see how I am doing because he is my friend. He gets a lot from the numbers. So, I want to go through the numbers today for him. Hopefully, he saw his name in the first line and decided to read more. My goal is to get him to actively invest some of his time in my adventure. Harvard Business School (HBS) graduates use a slightly different language, so I will write in their language and also try to translate. I am attempting to hike 2,190 miles in ninety days or less, so the math is 2,190 / 90 = 24.3. This means I have to hike an average of 24.3 miles a day or more to meet my goal. This is like my total sales for the day. I walk an average of three miles per hour so I have to hike a little more than an average of eight hours a day. Anything that I walk above 24.3 miles a day is profit. Anything below is a loss. I put all the profit or loss into what I am calling Banked Miles. You may think of it as a savings account. He will think of it as a reserve or the most important part of my balance sheet. I think of it as a reserve for a "rainy day." Right now, the number is negative (-11.7 miles) which means he probably would think twice about investing his time in me. I need to explain to him that it is just part of my initial start-up costs. I have a plan for the entire trip (which I have not shared with you) and although taking most of today off put me behind in my plan, I have a lot of time to make it up; and all good business people hide some "cushion" in their plan, just in case. My goal is to build up my banked miles (savings) quickly, as I do not like being overdrawn. I know New Hampshire and Maine are going to be hard, and that anything—like injury—can happen between here and there. So, 24.3 miles banked = one day. I can use it however I want. The biggest asset on my balance sheet is me, as I have to walk every mile. John has known me many years and knows my accomplishments and strengths and weaknesses. He can also read the "About" section for more specifics of the hike. My other assets include Mick and the van. All of these assets can quickly turn into liabilities if we have problems such as the van breaking down. The biggest liability on the balance sheet is the 90 days.

We woke today to an indescribable view of the Smoky Mountains from the Clingmans Dome parking overlook. From there I had to walk half a mile back to the Trail. Last evening I had to walk an additional half mile to the Dome Tower and another additional half mile back to the van. I also had to backtrack the other day one-quarter mile (times two), thinking I was lost. This is a total of two additional miles. Thru-hikers hate to do additional miles. You can think of this as a tax. So my tax on two hundred miles hiked divided by two extra miles equals one percent tax. Backpackers have to hike additional miles to water sources, shelters, towns to resupply, hostels, etc., so their tax is probably five percent to ten percent. I found a way of reducing my tax burden by doing a supported hike. Is that bad?

My business proposal to John is that he invests his time in my adventure as an active investor. This means I expect him to read the entire journal, add comments now and then of encouragement or questions, and maybe pay a visit to me somewhere on the Trail and bring me homemade cookies. Always ask for a little more than you can get (I would accept store-bought cookies from him). In return, he will get entertainment and a happy ending to my hike. The return on investment (ROI) is two times his time doing the above for three months. You cannot get a better deal for your time.

My short and easy hike today ended near Gatlinburg, Tennessee. I felt Mick needed a taste of real American culture and what better place than Dolly Parton's town. I think it has more pancake houses per square mile than anywhere in the world. Tomorrow is thirty-one difficult miles. . . .

The Forrest Gump comparison thing again? Really? You have seen my picture.

3 Comments

Sara

Only you would give a business pitch about your blog and hike! This is why I had to do one myself for that first cellphone! I miss you like crazy and I can't believe how fast you are eating up those miles. 200 in only 8–9 days, that's almost double the miles we did in England in the same amount of time. I hope you are feeling a bit rested and ready to tackle those 30 miles next. Love you and miss you!! —your favorite

Leroy

Tom, I have been following your progress but I have had no success in sending you two prior messages. This third attempt, hopefully, is a charm. Trek on and I look forward to seeing you next door in late August.

Leroy

Kate D.

Love this entry, Tom. I've already gotten a return on my investment <3 Keep on keepin' on!

A selfie in the Smokies during my ten-mile break.

Day 10: Goodbye Smoky Mountains

06/01/2017

Miles Hiked: 30.8

Total Miles: 237.9

Banked Miles: -5.2

I started a little after 6 a.m. as soon as there was light. The weather was perfect. After an initial climb, most of the morning hike was all at a height of between 5,500 feet and 6,500 along ridgelines. It was probably the most picturesque part of the Trail for me so far because I was so high (altitude) and there were few trees blocking the views both to my left and to my right. However, the clouds had burned off so you did not get the "smoky" feeling. Once we got to Clingmans Dome the other day, there has been a great mix of oak and pine trees on the mountains rather than mainly oak. The afternoon was a lot of downhill. It felt almost like the opposite of the big hike I did the other day entering the park—mainly descending today. The total climbing (elevation gain) for me today was 6,500 feet and the descent was 9,600 feet. Overall, the Smoky Mountains National Park was awesome and very well maintained. Everyone should come visit it at some point. There are a lot of day hike opportunities, as well as vistas you can see from your car. Mick hiked eight miles in to resupply me at my Mile 23, and we got back to our van at an unofficial-looking exit from the park at around 6 p.m. We then went to a nearby hiker hostel to take a shower. For those keeping score, this was shower number three. Shower number two was on Sunday at Fontana Dam. Mick made us "gluten free" pasta in the van for dinner. Really? I need carbs (it was actually very good and does have some carbs, I think).

My ten-day, two-hundred-plus mile health check-up: I think my fitness level has been really good. I have no issues on any of the climbs. My legs seem to start getting tired on mile twenty-three to twenty-four. I hope I can build up strength in them as I go. I have worked hard to keep my feet healthy. I let my feet air out every ten to thirteen miles, reapply my Hiking Goo, and then change my socks. I have not had any blisters so far (knock on wood), and my feet do not hurt. My knees are another story. The tendons in both my knees have started to get inflamed the last few days. It is quite uncomfortable. I have had to really slow down on the downhills. I am taking Advil, elevating them when I can, and now I am icing them in the van. Hopefully, I can work through this. I had this issue in Spain and worked through it. Other than that, my general health and mental health are really good.

I heard my father has not been feeling so good lately. Dad, I hope you are feeling better. I am thinking about you!

4 Comments

Marcie M

Way to go Tom! I hope your knees allow you to keep going at your crazy fast pace. Good Luck!!!

Uncle Kevin

Tom—you are doing incredibly well. As for the knees. Are you using hiking poles to shift some weight to your arms on the way down and somewhat on the way up? Uncle Gene and I are avid fans of them. Not only do they serve that purpose, they make stream crossings much easier. Time for ileotibial band stretches?

Rob Doo

Tom, 23 miles a day average....wow!!

Keep the carbs up. And we hope the tendon issue stays manageable.

Go, man, go!

Rob

Cedric

Hello Tom!

10 days hike at that pace is already an accomplishment. I just started reading you today as I was very busy the past few weeks. It sounds like a fun adventure and thank you for sharing it with us. I am sending you all the best for your knees. Hope your dad feels better soon.

Elisabeth and her family at the Trail finish at Springer Mountain.

Day 11: She Did It

Miles Hiked: 29.2
Total Miles: 267.1
Banked Miles: -0.3

06/02/2017

Today, I dedicate this post to my niece Elisabeth. On this beautiful day down south in Springer Mountain, GA, June 1, 2017, Elisabeth, at the age of nineteen, completed the entire Appalachian Trail going southbound starting at Mt. Katahdin in Maine (2,190 miles). Springer is where I started eleven days ago, going northbound. She went slowly these last couple days to ensure her whole family could be there at the finish. As all thru-hikers do, Elisabeth suffered various adversities and injuries, but she did not give up. She hiked the Trail for her own reasons, her own way, and with her own private, personal goals. This is an achievement that can never be taken away. She has now thru-hiked the Appalachian Trail and is an official member of the Appalachian Trail Conservancy (ATC) 2,000 Miles Club. From me and my family (and Mick) to Elisabeth and her family, we wish you congratulations. [Sorry for the late posting due to lack of Wi-Fi.]

One Comment

Catherine L

>Dear Tom, we cannot thank you enough for helping Elisabeth to embark on this journey last June when you attended Warren's AT school with her. We greatly appreciate all of your love, support and enthusiasm during this experience. Thinking of you every day and wishing you all the best in your journey! Xo, Cathy

My bad Climbing technique

Day 12: Hot Tub on the Trail

Miles Hiked: 22.9
Total Miles: 290
Banked Miles: -1.7

06/03/2017

Whaat are the odds? My knees were really hurting last night after twenty-nine miles, and we pull into Hot Springs, NC. I figured there had to be a hot spring somewhere in a town with this name. There was—The Hot Springs Resort and Spa. It was not really like a Ritz Carlton Resort and Spa. It was more like someplace from Dirty Dancing—not where Baby's family would go, more like where Patrick Swayze and his friends would go. For $40 you get an "all natural, mineral" private hot tub for eight overlooking the river for an hour—BYOB. It was just what the doctor ordered. This is after having the enormous Hiker Burger and tater tots ($9.99) and introducing Mick to meatloaf at the Smoky Mountain Diner. It was a memorable evening.

So, on a scale of tolerable, very painful, and excruciating, my knees are now down to 50 percent tolerable and 50 percent very painful. This is good news. I have been icing, elevating, and drugging them. What was the cause of the inflamed tendons? Well, what I have not told you in the posts is that through Georgia and into NC, "I was run'n" (another Forrest Gump quote). I know it was probably not smart to do when you are doing more than 2,000 miles, but I love to run (you understand this Lake Braddock Cross Country and DC Running Coach folks). I run every day at home, and I am good at it after thirteen years. I was only running the doable downhills—about 35–40 percent of the miles. I can't explain how fun it is to run, and even more fun down a mountain. It is very much like skiing without a chairlift or Helicopter (Paul) taking you back to the top. However, when I got to the longer, steeper, rockier mountains in NC, my knees decided that they had had enough. Going downhill was painful. Uncle Kevin commented about my use of my trekking poles going down to take some of the pounding—I did not use them while running except for balance, as in skiing. I have not run since. Case closed, right? Stop run'n. However, I just couldn't understand why the pain level changed so much, even by the hour. I noticed it was worst going down after climbing a really steep hill. Very long story (already) short, I figured out this afternoon that I was leaning way into the hill while climbing and it was that that was causing the pain. I had unknowingly changed my climbing technique when it got tougher. As soon as I changed it back—tolerable on the downhill. Hopefully, I will be better soon and this will be the last I discuss about my knees. The running? We will see.

3 Comments

JR R

Keep going Tom and stop running!! Save those knees for golf when you get back! JR

Jack Jr

Quicker recovery on your knees. Feel better soon.

I'm so sorry to hear that you were tortured with a hot tub and a hamburger. Be more careful next time!

Wendi

Hi Tom! This I Wendi!! I can not wait until you are in New Hampshire :)

Day 13: Fear of Heights

06/04/2017

Miles Hiked: 27.6

Total Miles: 317.6

Banked Miles: 1.6

It was a picture-perfect day. In fact, it was getting a little bit hot in the afternoon for the first time, with temperatures getting close to 80 degrees even in the elevation (2,500 to 4,500 feet today). It felt really nice with the cool breeze. All the flies and gnats and other annoying flying insects seemed to have chosen today to come out and play. So, I was hiking up and down numerous mountains and enjoying the varied flora and fauna (how is that Cedric?) when I came upon a sign. It said, Exposed Ridgeline Trail with an option below it to take the Bad Weather Trail. The former had a while blaze next to it and the latter a blue blaze. My hands immediately started to sweat. I had not seen a warning sign like this in the first 300 miles I had walked. I thought, "It must be really bad to put up a sign and offer an alternative route." So, when I saw the sign — fear. You see, I have a real fear of heights. So, you are thinking, "What is he doing hiking up and down mountains all day if he is afraid of heights?" Well, there are not too many places on the Trail supposedly that should invoke my fear. However, I worried this could be one of them. What scares me is places where there is a sheer wall (or drop) to my left, a very thin trail under me, and a precipitous drop to my right. My friends who have hiked with me before, for example in Patagonia, have seen this first hand. However, the sign is offering me an alternative to my fear. I could take the Bad Weather Trail on this beautiful day? If you are thru-hiking on the AT, you have to follow the white blaze (rectangle) the entire way. The Bad Weather Trail had a blue blaze. A blue blaze designates a side trail, like those leading to water sources. If you take a blue blaze, you have to come back to where you left the trail and go from there. But who would know? People even wrote on the sign things like there is no shame in taking the blue blaze. As Matt Damon's character said to the young boy in *Bagger Vance* when he penalized himself for the golf ball slightly moving when he removed a blade of grass, "I would know." So, off I went on the Exposed Ridgeline Trial — my hands sweating on my hiking poles. After worrying for 15 minutes while I climbed to the top, it turned out not to be scary. In fact, it was less scary and less difficult than the Billy Goat Trail in Potomac, MD. It just had some rocks to get over. Crisis averted. I saw the number 300 made from sticks a few miles up the trail. It was probably designating the 300 mile mark on the trail, but I imagined it as an invitation from the Brave 300 Spartans to join me because I was so brave.

I hiked with a person other than Mick today for the first time. It was a young man named John who just graduated with an engineering degree from Mercer College, and he was also doing a thru-hike attempt. He did not have a Trail name yet and was hoping someone would give him one. I also met a woman from England named Wandering Star yesterday who looked to be in her mid-sixties, carrying a full backpack. She told me this was her third time hiking the entire AT. Wow!

300 miles hiked or the Brave 300?

One Comment

Uncle Ken
  Tom, good for you conquering that decision point … and the ridgeline "trial"!

Day 14: The Scooby Doo Mobile

Miles Hiked: 24.6
Total Miles: 342.2
Banked Miles: 1.9

06/05/2017

Last night Mick parked the van, like most nights, at an AT road crossing where I finished that day. This one was called Sam's Gap. He was unable to park it flat as we were on a hill. I woke at around 2am feeling more tired than when I finished hiking. I think I was unconsciously using my legs to avoid falling on the floor from my bed because of the slight lean.

I got up at the normal 5:15 a.m., but today I was really tired from lack of sleep. However, I was up and out and on the Trail at around 6:15 a.m. It was a nice day with temperatures around 70 degrees, with thunderstorms predicted in the afternoon. The hike had a few steep climbs at the beginning, but nothing very difficult. At one point I tried to avoid a black pit of mud on the trail and put my foot between two rocks; and there stayed my shoe under the rocks as the momentum put my sock/foot right into the cold, wet, squishy mud. I looked around like a cat to see if anyone saw this (there was probably nobody within three miles), and as there was nobody to whine to about it, I balanced on my pole and bent down, got my shoe and put it on, and kept going. I got to the top of the mountain and it was a meadow with 360-degree views. This is only the second time I have gotten the Sound of Music-like grassy hillside. The other was at a place not too far back called Max Patch. I am usually on a forest trail so this is a treat. I got through around twenty-two miles with only around an hour to go and thought about how I dodged a bullet with the weather when I heard thunder. It was not a minute later when I got hit by torrential rain and wind. I had brought my very lightweight Boston Marathon rain jacket. It could not handle this kind of rain, but it did keep me warm. Funny thing, I did hear a little voice in my head saying, "Run, Forrest, run!" The rain and wind continued for around forty-five minutes as I continued. It is during a storm like this that you really appreciate the forest canopy you are under most of the time hiking the Trail. I was happy I was not out on that open meadow on the top of the mountain. Mick met me on the mountain under an umbrella when I was around fifteen minutes from the van and we hiked the rest of the way together. I was feeling great before the rain, but then I was wiped out completely when I reached the van an hour later.

I have not talked about our van much. It is really great. It is a RoadTrek 190 Popular that I rented on RVshare from a gentleman in North Carolina. There are two single beds in the back with a small table between them where I keep all my work stuff (laptop, printer, folders, and supplies) in a big Container Store plastic bin. Moving forward from the back is a little galley kitchen on the driver's side with a small stove, sink, refrigerator, microwave and plenty of storage. On the passenger side is a really small bathroom. There is a lot of storage above and below everything. There is a third seat behind the passenger seat where I often sit. We can stand upright in it no problem, but it is usually difficult for us both to be moving around at the same time. We have a retractable awning on the outside and four foldable chairs in the back. We have a generator, although we hardly use it as the battery meets most of our needs. We also have a Wi-Fi mobile hot spot as well as an antenna to get us better cell signal. The van has a lot of horsepower but is still small enough to get around on the small mountain roads where Mick needs to meet me. Although you may not believe this, it really doesn't stink (odor wise). Operations and maintenance of the van are pretty complicated and Mick is completely in charge of this and doing a great job. At 2 a.m. last night I put my mattress on the floor between the galley and the bathroom and slept there until morning as I had the kitchen wall to support me instead of my legs. Tonight the van is perfectly level at the Nolichucky River road crossing, now two weeks into our adventure.

Big Bald provided great views today.

4 Comments

Gramma

> Hi Tom.
>
> More than I expected, I am enjoying your detailed descriptions of your daily climbs but also the practical things: Van, mud, t-storms, —just like my favorite journal writers—you are exceeding expectations.
>
> Spoke to Elisha this evening about the "shyness" I have about this being shared. She said basically: say you would like to stay private.
>
> So hopefully, Gramma's comments are for you/Mick.
>
> We saw Aaron Judge at two Yankee games—he is good. Just returned from four days in Toronto—a good break from the rain at HL !
>
> Good speed ahead. . . . Thomas
>
> PS—thanks for your post about Elisabeth—well done.

Sue D

> I love this and you! Hike, Tommy, hike! It's so cool to read all your stories and follow your progress. Thank you for doing this and sharing your experiences!

Uncle Kevin

> Tom—you are doing absolutely amazingly fantastically well. Just keep in mind the fable of the tortoise and the hare, and the extra weight imposed on joints and tendons with that runnin'!
>
> Question. Do you use what I call scree or rock gaiters when you hike, or any gaiters? Gene and I use tall gaiters or short gaiters depending on when and where we are hiking. I think short would be fine for what you're doing. We like them for keeping crud out of our boots. They also give you a little impunity at stream crossings and with mud. But if you never pick up stones or dirt or twigs in your boots when you hike, there's not a need. It seems whenever I go out without gaiters I inevitably pick up a stone and have to stop and remove it from my boot. In any event, here's a link to what they look like. OR is a good product, as you probably know.
>
> https://www.campmor.com/c/outdoor-research-rocky-mountain-low-gaiters   same thing at REI, just costs more
>
> https://www.rei.com/search.html?q=gaiters&origin=web&ir=q%3Agaiters&page=1
>
> Nice scenery!

Jody

Hi Tom! I think back to the afternoon we spent in your kitchen years ago with your friends who had just hiked the AT, and can't believe you are taking on this challenge (actually, not true; I totally believe it!). My dad wants to visit you in Charlottesville and bring you supplies. I know the AT goes through Warwick, and I have a very close friend who has a house up there, so I'd love to meet you along the way, as well.

Much love and good health to you along the way! We are rooting for you!

Jody

Rainy Day

Day 15: Comments?

06/06/2017

Miles Hiked: 29.5

Total Miles: 371.7

Banked Miles: 7.1

We parked last night along the Nolichucky River. This sounds like a sequel to the Chucky horror movies I used to see advertised on TV. I was thinking that this one is about Chucky's evil cousin who comes out of the river and terrorizes hikers. Then, around 10 p.m., a car goes by and then turns around and parks behind us. A strange-looking guy with a lantern gets out, walks up to the van and knocks on our door (seriously, it happened).

My day was three hours and a break; then four hours and a break; then three hours and done. This gets me almost thirty miles. My breaks are getting a little longer lately as I do not want to push too hard. The first break was one hour and the second was forty-five minutes. The morning was clear, but rain was predicted. I felt lethargic for the first phase of the hike. I felt like I was just wrapping myself around and around the mountain climbing up the outside of the first mountain like a piece of thread on a spool. The hike got more and more enjoyable as the day continued. Mick met me around 4 miles from the end of the hike and we walked out together. It started raining again when I was around one and a half hours from the finish. Rain had been predicted all day, so I got off easy. What I really need is a weather forecast I can count on like I get at home from my friend Jay's team at WUSA 9 News. Tomorrow I go back to the higher elevations and it's supposed to be beautiful.

I want to pass on my congratulations to my nephew and nieces who are recently graduating. My brother's son Ian graduated high school with honors and will be attending Cornell in the fall. Elisabeth's sister, Courtney, also graduated high school with many honors and will be attending Amherst College in the fall. My brother's daughter Anna graduated from University of Chicago with Honors and has a job at the FX Channel in L.A. as an assistant to the president (think *Devil Wears Prada*, only much nicer). I wish I could have attended your graduations. The apples fell far from my tree with these three.

Finally, I really appreciate all your comments on the site. I have heard that there were issues with leaving comments, so I had my website developer Brian make some fixes. Hopefully, it works better now. I have to approve all comments before they go up on the site, which can sometimes take a little time. I have approved all of them so far, although Jon's was right on the borderline as usual. Let me know if you want me to discuss certain things in my journal that I might be neglecting.

2 Comments

Catherine L

Hi Tom! Just took my my Nat'l Geo AT maps and AWOL book back off the shelf to follow your journey. I was having withdrawal after E finished last week! I wrote a note in the margin at mile 382 saying that there were 40–55 mph winds with 80 mph gusts when she was hiking where you will be tomorrow. Hoping you have more pleasant weather!! Take care of those knees. Thanks for the shout-out for Courtney!

Xo, Cathy

Kate

Nice Channel 9 shout-out, Tom! And I'm impressed to see your banked miles growing by the day—yay, you!

One of the many brilliant views in the Roan Highlands.

Day 16: Goodbye NC

Miles Hiked: 25
Total Miles: 396.7
Banked Miles: 7.8

06/07/2017

I started a little later than usual (7:15) this morning as I was hoping the clouds would burn away for some great views as I climbed Roan Mountain to a height of 6,200 feet. It would be the last time in the 6,000s until New Hampshire. The hike to the top was relatively easy (not too steep) but there were no views because of the clouds/fog. Oh well, there will always be another time.

I hate to say goodbye to North Carolina. I really like this state. Many of my relatives live in NC, mainly in Wilmington—the Trasks and the Halls—and they are great people. My sister Jenn recently moved from Charlotte to L.A. (Orange County) with her job at Sidney Frank Imports. We used to have an office in Raleigh during my tech company days (3GI). My whole family, including my parents, my brother John's family, and Jenn, spent many summers together at Wrightsville Beach and Bald Head Island. I am very close to Boone, North Carolina right now and it is where my whole family spent a week in 2013 at a house I won at a charity auction for the Starlight Children's Foundation. I remember entering the Bear Mountain Race five miles straight up Grandfather Mountain that my brother John helped encourage me to enter. I got to run through the Scottish Highland Games (we are Clan MacGregor) with bagpipes playing on the way to the top where John and his son Ian were cheering me on at the finish. It was our last family trip. Oh well, there will always be another time.

I met Mick at the van after seven miles and got ready for the next fifteen-mile stretch. The cool breeze was blowing hard today, so I decided to put on my long-sleeve shirt from the Bear race. North Carolina did not disappoint, of course. Of the first four hundred miles on the AT, I had the most spectacular views by far today. The area is known as the Roan Highlands and probably ten miles of the fifteen miles were out of the forest and on exposed meadows some 5,500 to 5,800 feet high with 360-degree panoramic views. Wow. If you want to do a long day-hike, Carver Gap to 19E in NC should be on your list. The only thing that I am sure of on this hike of the AT is that every day and every mile is something new.

One final note: as I was walking through NC, I was thinking about why people would be interested in reading my journal. I also thought about the fact that NC is the NASCAR capital of the US. Why do people like to watch NASCAR? It is for the crashes. There is still plenty of time and opportunity for me to crash on this journey, so keep reading. . . .

Goodbye, NC!

4 Comments

Bobby M

Tom, I am with you and now looking forward to reading your posts—you are a Rockstar...

Linda

Loving your blog. I'm curious about how your boots are holding up with all the rain?

Tom S

Thomas,

Unbelievable! Hiking almost a marathon every day. I've got to sit down and rest just thinking about that concept! I certainly am following and enjoying your adventure. Might there be another book to be written this time regarding your AT trip?

Looking at what you have accomplished on the AT to date and thinking back to our doubles tennis-playing heydays, I'm not sure why our opponents always called you "Creampuff" during our matches. I distinctly remember them saying "We are glad to be playing you guys because Tom is a Creampuff." Oh, wait a minute, do you think there's any chance they were talking about me and not you? Whatever!!

Two states down, twelve to go. Despite the onset of Summer, I feel there's a "Cool Breeze" heading my way to Virginia. Continued success in your pursuit and stay healthy.

One of the TOM-TOMs

Alexandra D

Did you know that the *Last of the Mohicans* was filmed in NC? Do you have enough Celtic music for your journey? Wendi and I are enjoying your trip [vicariously].

Stream near Hampton, Tenn.

Day 17: Now Streaming

06/08/2017

Miles Hiked: 30.1

Total Miles: 426.8

Banked Miles: 13.6

I started my hike in cool 57-degree air at a little past 6 a.m. I walked along and above beautiful mountain streams in sunshine much of the day, when I was not in the forest. It had a calming effect. I have not had to walk through any streams like I will in New Hampshire and Maine. All the stream crossings here have bridges or well-placed rocks. There were not as many panoramic mountain views today, but after yesterday, I felt I had my quota for a while. My day was broken into two-, five-, and three-hour walks. To keep me honest, the Trail threw in a big mountain climb at the end of the day. It was three miles up and then three miles down. When I got to the top, I decided to call my Mom and then Alex (our GM at Medium Rare in Capitol Hill) as I get the best reception at the tops of mountains, and I only had the downhill to complete my thirty miles. After two nice conversations, I headed down. Unfortunately, it was a false peak and I still had twenty more minutes of climbing (ugh!). When I got to the real top at 5 p.m., the sky started turning dark, so I decided to hightail it down. No rain came.

Knees update: I am happy to report that my right knee is 100 percent and my left is 80 percent. I only took Advil once yesterday and none today. It is amazing that one slight change to my walking technique, that I did not notice I had changed, made such a difference. I am sure if my Uncle Kevin or Uncle Gene had seen me climbing, they would have spotted the problem early as they are hiking pros. It is like when you are playing golf and you keep slicing the ball out of bounds and your left elbow hurts. You go to your pro, like my Aunt Nancy and Uncle Roger. They watch you and tell you to turn your foot three inches to the right; and then all of us sudden you are hitting everything straight and your elbow no longer hurts. At Medium Rare, even the smallest changes anywhere in the process of making our Secret Sauce will cause the sauce to taste wrong or not the same. I have had a running coach the last 8 years, Mike Hamberger (DCRunningCoach.com). Among other things, he helps me stay consistent with my technique to avoid injury and to get faster (and he builds me training plans) which I believe has been a key element to my success so far on this hike. A final example, Cedric Maupilliar is arguably the best chef in Washington

D.C. (visit Convivial). He is well trained in cooking technique, but if he ever wants to beat me in golf (and I am terrible) and ensure he does not injure himself or anyone else, he needs to work a lot more on his golf technique. Thank you for the concern about my knees—I am feeling pretty good now.

4 Comments

Sue D

What a marketer! Now I'm Jonesing for some Medium Rare secret sauce! And for Convivial. (Not for a running coach though.) Glad your knees are better!

Maggie G

Dear Tom,

Jia You!

Proud of u !

Maggie

Jody

Hi Tom! Watching your progress in amazement! Thinking about you every step of the way!

Jody

Hey Tom! I've been trying to post for days now, but getting error messages for some reason; hoping this will work! We've been watching your progress in amazement, and although I can't believe you are really doing this, I can absolutely believe that you are doing it! Keep it up the good work and stay safe!

Lots of love,

Jody

Can bears get into vans?

Day 18: Where is the bear?

Miles Hiked: 30.7

Total Miles: 457.5

Banked Miles: 20

06/09/2017

I started another big mile day by a "dam" lake called Watauga. It reminded me of Burke Lake by my house, except a lot of it was closed because of bear activity. It's one of those strange things—you want to see a bear, but you also hope it doesn't attack you when you do encounter it. I met a thru-hiker yesterday who had already seen four bears. He had seen one yesterday just twenty minutes before I got to the same place. As I was walking by the dam, I talked to a couple who had just seen a bear, a few minutes before I arrived, "scamper across the road." These same nice local people also told me that they had met Jennifer Pharr Davis, the current female Appalachian Trail supported hiking record holder (forty-five days), during her record attempt a couple years ago—at the same place they met me today. It made me feel good for some reason—not sure why. She has written some very good books about hiking the Trail if you are interested in that sort of thing. The second part of my hike was sixteen miles of ridgeline. It was short ups and downs for over five hours; still no bears. It was all sunshine today, probably in the low 70s. It threatened to storm a few times during the remainder of my hike, but it did not. When I start hiking tomorrow morning, I will be in the same place I was last year when I saw my first bear on the Trail. Maybe he will be there again, "Hey, aren't you that hiker from last year? I should have eaten you then."

If you want to get a better visual idea of the terrain, Mick's meet-ups, and what my day is like, here is the link to Karl Meltzer's video of his record-breaking supported hike last year. The big differences are that he is hiking probably fifteen to sixteen hours a day (fifty miles per day); he is going north to south; he is in a station wagon and not a luxury RV like me; he doesn't have time to go out to dinner and write a journal entry at the end of the day. http://atrun.redbull.com/karl-meltzer-appalachian-trail-13/p/1

Chef Mick's dinner in the van tonight.

Here is a view of my route so far almost to Virginia.

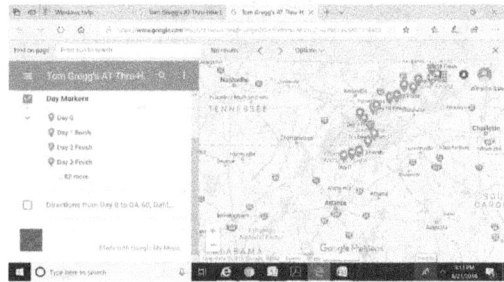

4 Comments

Steve

Tom,

Twenty Banked miles! Very impressive.

So proud of you!

Steve

Kate

Hi Tom! I hear bears like pickles, so you better make sure you cleaned up well after dinner! It looks like you'll be in meet-up range soon, so I'll reach out to Lish to see when/how we might be able to do a few miles with you if the stars align. Then again, we'd probably slow you down—30.7 miles today! Dang!

Catherine L

Hello again! You are right where Elisabeth did her ultra hike day. She hiked from Watauga Lake to Damascus, 42 miles, in a 24 hour period in early May. She originally was going to hike two 21-mile days with her co-hiker Dan, aka trail name "Dad." They hiked from 10:30am until 1 am, went to sleep and then she woke up freezing cold before dawn and knew she wouldn't be able to go back to sleep. So she packed up and started hiking again. She arrived into Damascus right at 10:30 a.m. Just wanted to see if she could do it! From what I hear, you will like Damascus. Stop and eat some good food! Xo, Cathy. P.S., Not sure if she saw any bears!

Sue D

Made me think of this joke: Two men were walking through the woods when a large bear walked out into the clearing no more than 50 feet in front of them. The first man dropped his backpack and dug out a pair of running shoes, then began to furiously attempt to lace them up as the bear slowly approached them. The second man looked at the first, confused, and said, "What are you doing? Running shoes aren't going to help, you can't outrun that bear." "I don't need to," said the first man, "I just need to outrun you."—Happy bear sightings! Be beary careful!

Sara Beara.

Day 19: Bears! Bye TN hi VA

Miles Hiked: 28.4
Total Miles: 485.9
Banked Miles: 24.1

06/10/2017

I have so much to share today. I started hiking at 6 a.m. on an eleven-mile hike into Damascus, VA. I had just gotten off the phone with my business partner Steve (while hiking) discussing the construction of the new Arlington Medium Rare when I heard a loud rustling in the leaves. I quickly got my phone back out and started looking around. To my right, about fifteen or twenty yards away in almost the exact area I saw a bear last year, I saw two little bear cubs start to climb a tree. Mama bear was below them on the ground. When the cubs saw me, they quickly climbed much higher. I am guessing Mama Bear wanted to say to me, "Hey Cool Breeze, welcome back. I want to introduce you to my two cubs Sara and Caroline." I was thinking to say back, "Wow, I have two older cubs with the same names." Anyway, as I was trying to take a picture, Caroline Cub decided to climb even higher so as not to have to be in the picture. Then I thought, Mama bears probably do not like it when someone causes their cubs to climb that high in the trees, so I decided to quickly move on, excitedly. These were my first bears on the hike.

Meanwhile, back at the van, another bear decided to make a visit while Mick was getting ready. According to Mick, the bear did a detailed inspection of the outside of the van. From his description it sounds like it was Robbie or Lindy Bear from my childhood asking, "Can Tommy come out and play?" As Mick would not reply, it left heading north on the AT looking for me (see picture below).

Today, I said goodbye to Tennessee. Everyone was very hospitable. I did not have much background with TN before the hike. Much of my time in TN was just going through it to get somewhere else. My fondest memory of the state was when my Dad and I were driving through on college visits. I wanted to go to school in the south where it was warm. We were on our way to visit SMU, my eventual choice, when we stopped at a gas station. The attendant said, "Lady or unlady?" We said, "What?" After some thought and discussion, we figured out he was asking if we wanted leaded or unleaded gas. From that point on, we only spoke in a southern drawl for the rest of the trip. To this day, I still call my father, Pa, and he calls me boy because of the time in Tennessee.

We entered my home state Virginia today. We will be in VA for over five hundred miles. It feels good to be home. I went to the Appalachian

Trail Institute (ATI) with Elisabeth here in Damascus, VA, around this time last year. This is why I had already met the bear. It was during a practice hike. I have actually already hiked the entire trail I hiked today. Many people say that Virginia is the easiest part of the trail. This is not true. It is long and hard. I have been working with Mick on his southern drawl. We have been using the phrase, "W'rs d B'r? Over Th'r." or Where is the bear? Over there.

Robbie / Lindy Bear heading north on AT.

Wild Ponies at Grayson Highlands State Park (VA).

Day 20: The Grayson Highlands

06/11/2017

Miles Hiked: 24.1

Total Miles: 510

Banked Miles: 23.9

I think the song goes something like, "But I could walk five hundred miles, and I could walk five hundred more. . . ." Yes, I reached five hundred miles on my twentieth day. I also made my first big directional error. I use the best phone app for the Trail. It is called Guthook. It is really great. It utilizes GPS so you do not need a phone signal. I can see if I am ten feet off the trail at any time. It is what allows me to tell you my exact ascent and descent numbers. I know how far away I am from anything at any time. I was walking towards the Grayson Highlands this morning when I came across a group of fifteen or twenty scouts. They were sitting on the Trail resting. I went around them to the left and proceeded on the Trail. A while later I noticed I had not seen any white blazes in a while. I took out my smartphone to look at my Guthook app to check my location and the little blue arrow was nowhere near the Trail (Arghh). I had walked 1.7 miles the wrong way. That is 3.4 miles roundtrip. It was also a hard trail, with a ton of rocks and roots. I was close to getting back when I saw another two thru-hikers and informed them they were also not on the Trail. The scouts were still there when I got back almost 1.5 hours later. They were still sitting in front of the sign and the turn uphill. Oh well, that is a 3.4-mile stupid tax on me that I had to pay for not looking for the white blazes; so, I really walked 27.5 miles today.

Grayson Highlands is billed as one of the most scenic spots on the AT and it did not disappoint. It is known for beautiful meadows, panoramic mountain views and wild ponies. Also today, the wild rhododendrons were in bloom. It is Saturday and the state park has a lot of parking, so there were many people out for a day hike. Today was also the first day that I felt I was getting a lot of sun. I think I liked the Roan Highlands a few days ago a little better, but both were great. The hike overall was long and hard. It was hard because I felt I was walking on rocks and roots all day. As my shoes are lightweight trail running shoes and not hiking boots, my feet start to really feel beaten-up by the end of the day. Score one for hiking-boot fans. Hiking boots will get a lot of points when I get to Pennsylvania.

I met an Army veteran thru-hiker today (the one also walking the wrong way above) with quite the war record and many purple hearts. He had to get off the trail today because of an administrative problem with his retirement pay that he could not solve from the Trail and probably could not be solved quickly. The fact that he could walk five hundred miles with all the injuries he sustained over five deployments (and six IEDs) was amazing. The fact that he had to leave the Trail because of an administrative glitch in the retirement system was heartbreaking.

Cool Breeze at five hundred miles.

2 Comments

Kit L

Hey CB,

Foot pain is common no matter what shoes you wear. The "hiker hobble" gets every one. Just make sure you pay attention to your shoe's mileage. Age doesn't matter for a shoe, only mileage. Your shoes are designed to last around 250 miles.

I hope you are still having fun!

Don't Matter

Grace

Beautiful scenery in the Highlands, ponies and all and what a view, for the bear "man sighting!" It must be equally captivating, the sights "and" the sounds…

The wonder of it all!

Fresh water.

Day 21: Be careful what you wish for

Miles Hiked: 31
Total Miles: 541
Banked Miles: 30.6

06/12/2017

A COOL BREEZE ON THE APPALACHIAN TRAIL 65

So, it was 8:15 a.m., and I had been walking for about two hours when I heard the heavy rustling of the leaves again. I was on a three-foot wide flat trail on the side of a mountain. To my left was a downhill slope that would be hard to run down, but you could probably slide, and the same slope upwards to my right. I started to get out my phone/camera as I went around a curve, and up onto the trail from below, just ten feet in front of me, a bear. He did not see me, so I quickly started to sing in a baritone, "De Da Da Da Da," to make him aware of my presence. He looked at me for a second and ran up the hill. At the same time, I heard a squeal like a pig and a second bear started running down the hill. I then look forward left and saw a little cub climbing a tree as fast it could. Then, I looked down the trail in front of me. About thirty yards ahead was a bear standing on two legs, around my same height, and looking right at me. Wow! I continued to sing loudly the same tune, so they knew exactly where I was, and I started to move back around the curve out of the sight of the big bear. I could see the cub come down from the tree from where I was standing. I remained in the same spot singing for around two to three minutes. Then, I cautiously continued, as I had to keep walking north. The bears had either moved on or had done a good job hiding, as I did not see them again. On a scale of "any turbulence on a plane flight" being a ten, this was probably a two for me on the fear factor. I felt that I had a level of control over the situation. However, if this occurs again, we may have to change my trail name to Brown Shorts. As I continued walking and was replaying everything back in my mind, I tried to figure out what I was singing. Then it hit me. It was the notes played in the Richard Dreyfuss 1970s movie *Close Encounters of the Third Kind*, when they were trying to communicate with the aliens (I can't make this stuff up). Oh, I did not get a picture. . . .

The remainder of the day was a pleasant walk in bright sunshine (in the low 80s) which was much more sympathetic on my feet (fewer rocks and roots). I did Medium Rare work during my breaks. It was all good today.

2 Comments

Jennifer G

Thinking about you every day and how proud I am of your accomplishments! Love the bears and all the great views. Also, you have inspired me to start hike/walk/jogging every day. I am doing at least 3-4 miles a day in your honor.

Love you,

Jenn Jenn

P.S. You are missing the new *Bachelorette* and all the drama with the *Bachelor in Paradise* filming. Watching isn't the same without you.

Alexandra D

I told you that if you get eaten by a bear that I won't forgive you!

Day 22: 25% of the Trail completed

06/13/2017

Miles Hiked: 28.2
Total Miles: 569.3
Banked Miles: 34.6

It was another very nice day on the Appalachian Trail. It was the first day I started to see more northbound thru-hikers. I knew I would eventually catch up, so today might as well have been the day. I think I have seen an average of maybe one or two a day up to now, but today I probably saw fifteen people thru-hiking. I met a group of four thru-hikers at a shelter. We talked for a few minutes, and I kept going. A few minutes later I saw one them (Mouse King) coming up from behind. Nobody has passed me in twenty-two days. We started hiking up a five hundred foot climb together, and I could not keep up with him, and he was wearing a heavy backpack. Keep in mind that this is not a race. However, I figured if he beat me to the top, I would catch him on the downhill because nobody is faster than I am on the downhill (and it is not a race). Well, he beat me down the mountain too. To celebrate his victory, Mick and I invited the Mouse King and his hiking companion Trailian to have some trail magic (sodas, chips, apples, and chocolate) from the van. Sometimes, not racing and trail magic help you through some of the monotony of hiking long hours. I still had a big 2,000 foot climb to do after the "not race," and I flew up the mountain feeling good the whole way. We are staying in a little parking lot area tonight called Walker's Gap and Chef Mick is making us some omelets to celebrate having completed 25 percent of the trail. Did that go fast?

Mick is requesting a trail name change. He wants to keep the "Mick" part, but he wants to change Dundee to Sherpa. He wants to be "Mick Sherpa" because he feels he plays the role of a Sherpa on the hike. I think that we should change it to "Mick Shaggy" or just "Shaggy" because he drives the Scooby Doo Mobile (van) and I think there is a striking resemblance to the cartoon character. See the pictures below. We should put it to a vote?

Mick

Shaggy

5 Comments

Catherine L
    McSherpa is my vote!

Uncle Ken
    Congrats on hitting the 25 percent mark. Go, Cool Breeze, Go!

Alexandra D
    Mick is looking pretty good.

Jon
    vote: Mick Sherpa

    Impressive to watch your pace Tom. Really good going. Looking forward to our meet up (unless you get too far ahead) for forum mtg at my farm. Hope that still happens. Pool/hot tub/cold beer.... Glad to hear my last post came as close to the edge without being censored.

Uncle Ken
    Tom, regarding trail name, consider you are on a 30 mile hike and are counting on someone to locate the van at the next trail head, hike in 10 miles to meet you with food and water, and accompany you the rest of the way. Would you rather depend on "Mick Sherpa" or "Shaggy"?

From left to right: Autumn Leaf, Giggles, and Wombat.

Day 23: Meeting more thru hikers

Miles Hiked: 29.4

Total Miles: 598.7

Banked Miles: 39.7

06/14/2017

A short time after getting started this morning on the first leg of a four-leg hiking day, I saw another bear, ho-hum. This, my eighth bear, was a solo-hiking bear, fully supported like me, also heading north on the Trail. I got out my phone to take a picture, but it was still on selfie mode from my quarter-of-the-way picture from yesterday. The bear saw me and decided to leave the Trail quickly down the hill. The second leg of my hike today (ten miles) ended in a big rain storm. I did not bring my jacket because it was so hot that I thought any rain would feel good. This was more rain than I expected, though, and was totally soaked. I had my Crest Cleaner bag keeping my little pack dry. I took a long one-and-a-half hour break after that in the van. It was getting near the end of the day on my last leg of the hike, and I was thinking I had not seen any thru-hikers today. I thought perhaps there are hiker clusters and I hit one yesterday. Then, I saw a hiker ahead of me. Her trail name was Giggles and she told me she had hiked the entire Pacific Crest Trail (PCT) last year. I then came upon Wombat from Germany and his girlfriend Autumn Leaf from Mexico. I invited them all back to the van for Trail magic. Mick put the awning of the van out as it started drizzling again, and we put our four folding chairs out, and we had a great time learning about our new friends on the Trail. These three are doing a lot of miles each day, so it is possible we may see them again. This was a fun way to end the day. The gnats and flies are getting really bad (buzzing my ears), so I am going to have to buy some spray and hope it helps. Mick Sherpa seems to be winning the vote so far. . . .

2 Comments

Matt

Tom—looks like you are doing great! I just caught up on your posts from the last few days. You look way too clean-shaven to be on this hike...the conspiracy theorists are wondering. Matt.

Bill & Laura Ann

Laura Ann and I are following your journey and enjoying your comments. So impressed!!! Keep it up. How do you not have a long beard by now???

Sara and me on the Camino in Spain with Mick in 2015.

Day 24: Happy Birthday Sara

Miles Hiked: 35.5
Total Miles: 634.2
Banked Miles: 50.9

06/15/2017

I want to start by saying that I have the two best daughters in the whole world. If anyone writes a comment disputing this fact, I will not approve it. Today is my older daughter Sara's twentieth birthday. I am very sad that I am not home to celebrate with her. My biggest regret in hiking the Appalachian Trail is that I am not hiking it with her. You see, she is my hiking partner. We hiked all of the one hundred-mile Cotswold Way in England together when she was sixteen, and then when she turned eighteen, we hiked the five hundred-mile Camino De Santiago in Spain together. This is where we met Mick. These two hikes with her were two of my all-time favorite experiences. On our hikes, we talked a lot about a lot of things, including hiking the Appalachian Trail together. However, she is a very busy young lady now with a summer job at a geo-political consulting firm in Georgetown, and in the fall she will be attending Sciences Po in Paris. She is also more interested in doing the Trail by the more traditional backpacking method. I felt a need to do this hike now, in a supported method, so we are not doing this together, which is very sad for both of us. However, I think of Sara often when I hike and I thought of her even more today. Today there were some steep, difficult, long hills to climb. Sara and I had a saying, "What goes up must keep going up, and then go up some more, and then finally up even higher, and then straight down." Sara could always beat me up the hills. She has another gear that I do not have. I thought today that if I were to give her a trail name, it would be "No Boy Good Enough." She might not want this one. . . . Anyway, I hiked a few extra miles today in her honor. I am now averaging a little more than a marathon a day. Happy birthday Sara—I love you.

2 Comments

Sara
> I love you Dad! Thanks for the post and those extra miles! I miss you a ton and am sad I'm not out there with you. I laughed out loud at that trail name. Very "Dad move" of you. I had a great birthday today and getting to talk to you was one of the best parts. I'm so proud of how well you are doing on the AT so far. I will always be your #1 cheerleader and forever your hiking partner! Love, —Sara

Jack Jr.
> Great post today Tom

Cool Breeze and Poppins.

Day 25: Hiked with Poppins

Miles Hiked: 27.5
Total Miles: 661.7
Banked Miles: 53.3

06/16/2017

I started late today (around 7:15 a.m.) after my long day yesterday. I met a young man at the beginning of my hike named Poppins (think umbrella). I hiked with Poppins the first twenty-three miles of the day. This is the first time on the AT that I hiked with someone all day. Poppins recently graduated from University of Maine with a degree in Chemical Engineering and now hopes to go on to vet school in Colorado. He is carrying a pack and trying to do the Trail in one hundred days. He is the fastest unsupported hiker I have met. He is also a trail runner and has already run a fifty-mile race. The funny thing was he told me that he has always wanted to be a dishwasher in a restaurant. I have never heard "always wanted to be" and "dishwasher" in the same sentence. Have you heard this before Alex, Chris, Vanessa, or Paulos (my Medium Rare general managers)? If he wasn't going to Colorado, we could probably make a dishwasher position open for him at Medium Rare.

He stopped for the night a shelter along the trail and I continued on for another four miles. It was four miles, no big deal. Well, this turned-out to be an extremely difficult four miles for me. There were no up or downs. It was four miles of rocks. These were not fun boulders you hop from one to another, these were rocks of all sizes protruding from the ground. There was no place to put your foot down comfortably for four miles. On top of trying to balance and the pain from the sharp ends of each rock on each step, I had to use my left hand exclusively to knock the gnats out of my face. I think it was one of the most miserable times that I have had so far—right after a fun day walking with Poppins. It took several hours for my feet to stop hurting enough to write this (I do not have an Internet connection so I won't be able to publish this until tomorrow anyway). I looked in my notes from the ATI school, and it said this was going to be a rocky section, but I had not checked it. I have to figure out how to do better with the rocks and bugs as I get further north.

One Comment

Tom S

Tom,

I see you are just up the road from Mountain Lake, which of course was made famous because that's where the original "Dirty Dancing" movie was filmed. Any sightings of "Baby" (and I don't mean bears)?

Following every day and continue to be amazed. Stay physically and mentally strong! And enjoy!

Tom S.

Simple but good. Hmmm.

Day 26: This is hard

06/17/2017

Miles Hiked: 24.6

Total Miles: 686.3

Banked Miles: 54.4

Well, I am down here in Southwest Virginia pretty close to Blacksburg and Virginia Tech for all you Hokies fans. I am telling you, this has been the hardest part of the Trail so far for me. I am really good at the endurance part of the Trail. I can climb forever. However, every day here seems to present a new challenge. Couple that with the heat, humidity, and bugs, and it is hard. I was going to try to hike more than thirty-two miles today, but the first twenty-four miles took me so long to complete and my feet were so tired that I decided to call it a day at 5:30. The rain in the afternoon today actually helped to keep the bugs away, but it made some of the way a lot slipperier. I think the rain also kept a lot of hikers undercover, as I only saw one thru-hiker actually hiking today. There is another hiker on the trail with the name Cool Breeze (young guy in his twenties). However, this guy is what is known as a "yellow blazer". This means he catches rides to the next hostel and pretends that he has hiked and then parties with all the hikers at each hostel (yellow for the lines on the road). I do not like sharing my name with this guy as people will get confused and think I am not really hiking thru-hiking.... We decided to take the "The" that Facebook dropped and add it to Mick's new trail name: He is now Mick The Sherpa.

Mick and I drove from where I finished today to the town of Catawba, where I will hike to tomorrow, to get some Internet connection and a phone signal. We were also told by some other hikers that there was a must-go to restaurant there called The Homeplace. We just finished dinner there and it was good, southern fare. The place was packed. I think there were more cars in the parking lot than the population of the town. The concept was that you only had to choose ham or roast beef to go with your fried chicken. Everything else was included. It was a simple, *prix fixe* menu. What a great idea.

I saw another bear today.... This makes nine since I entered Virginia. This bear was walking up onto to the Trail around 3:30 p.m. He probably thought no hiker was dumb enough to be at the top of the mountain in the rain at that time. He was around twenty feet in front of me and did not see me at first. As I went for the camera, he saw me and took off back down the hill.

3 Comments

Grace L

Keep on Tommy, we are cheering you!

Rob D

Tom

Congratulations on hitting the one-fourth way mark! What an awesome thing. I'm following along with you each day and it's exhausting!

Rob

JR R

Stay with it Tom! You've got the endurance and stamina to make it through any part of the Trail and in any weather!

JR

Dinner with fellow thru-hikers.

Day 27: Dragons Tooth

Miles Hiked: 21.4
Total Miles: 707.7
Banked Miles: 51.5

06/18/2017

I was more than a little nervous starting the day. I would be hiking Dragons Tooth. I wrote in my *Data Book* from my Appalachian Trail Institute (ATI) school that it will be a "big issue for me." This means that it could be a fear of heights issue for me. In my true fashion, I decided I would worry about it a lot last night and the first seven miles this morning. What if I can't do it? Dragons Tooth was about six miles in on my second leg of the day. As I started walking the second leg, I had a burst of energy, and I just flew up the first mountain and then flew up towards Dragons Tooth. Very few people could have probably kept up with me. I decided if I hiked really hard, I would be too tired to worry. I had Mick walk in from the next road crossing and go through the difficult sections of Dragons Tooth before I got there to see how hard it was. Mick was really sweating when I saw him and he said it was going to be hard. Uh oh! In my head I could see a monolith rock looking like a dragon jutting out over the side of a cliff, and I would have to climb it and inch my way across with my back against its dragon rock nostrils. Anyway, it turns out that it was just a rock scramble. The most I could fall was probably ten feet and maybe twist an ankle. Mind you, it was the hardest spot on the Trail so far, but I am not afraid of this kind of rock scramble. When finally done, I was quite relieved. If I was to do it again, I would probably enjoy it. I got in the van and called Kit (Don't Matter) in Williamsburg. I told him I was climbing McAfee Knob (see Day 0 pic.) and Tinker Cliffs tomorrow which is a half-mile cliff walk which I also wrote "big issue" in my book. He told me it was nothing to worry about, so I am going to believe him—I will tell you tomorrow if he is an honest man. . . . I only did twenty-one miles today because the next road crossing is twenty miles farther.

Because I got done early, I was already back at the van when a huge thunderstorm hit. We decided to put out our awning and chairs to help hikers stuck in the rain. First, there was a family from South Korea out for a quick hike, and got stuck in the storm. Then from the mountain came some fellow thru-hikers that we had already met on the trail. There was Bourne (from New Zealand), Pixie, and CB. We ended up driving back to the same restaurant as last night but this time our group was nine thru-hikers when we finally sat down to eat. This group could eat—wow!

One Comment

Sue D

This trail is no walk in the park. . . . Who knew? Nice work, Tommy! Keep scrambling!!!

My family.

Day 28: Happy Father's Day

06/19/2017

Miles Hiked: 21.8

Total Miles: 729.5

Banked Miles: 49

Happy Father's Day Dad, and sorry I could not come for a visit. I hope to see you in around a week. This was quite a day. The highlight was my family coming to visit me. This was the first visit I have received. I knew my wife was coming, but I did not know my girls would also be here (and our dog Cosmo). It was so great seeing them. We met at the Peaks of Otter Lodge on the Blue Ridge Parkway and we had a great dinner. They brought me new socks, shoe inserts, and bug spray among other things.

We were going to meet at 4 p.m., so I knew I had to start early this morning on my hike. I left the van at around 5:45 a.m. with a four-mile hike to McAfee Knob. This is the place in the picture for my Day 0 entry. Mick came with me because he wanted to see the famous Knob. I got closer to the ledge than I thought I would. Mick sat on the ledge. Our view was obscured by the clouds, but it was still cool. After some pictures, I started on the next sixteen miles of the twenty-mile first leg. A few miles in I got to the Tinker Cliffs, which I mentioned yesterday. Kit (Don't Matter) is an honest man, but perhaps his memory is not as reliable anymore. The trail on the cliffs did take me close to edge—OK, right to the edge on several occasions. The good news was that I could step off safely to my right if needed. However, I stayed on the Trail and powered through it. I finished the first twenty miles around 1 p.m. and decided to just do two more miles so I could get cleaned-up before the visit. I have had a few lower mileage days, so I need to start picking it up.

As close as I got to the edge at McAfee Knob.

One Comment

CB

So glad you got to see the whole fam for Father's Day! Keep that breeze blowin'!
—CB

I am 1/3 of the way

Day 29: 1/3 of the way

Miles Hiked: 37.6
Total Miles: 767.1
Banked Miles: 62.3

06/20/2017

I started the hike late today at 8 a.m. We stayed at Peaks of Otter Lodge last night. This was my first night not sleeping in the van. I was not sure how I was going to respond after seeing my family yesterday. I guess the answer was that they also brought me a huge amount of energy (and eighteen pairs of new socks). I was flying this morning and all day. I reached the one-third of the way point around five minutes into my hike. So, I really got there in twenty-eight days. I was hiking pretty close to the Blue Ridge Parkway a lot of the day which meant I could meet up with Mick and the van a lot. I would do a mile or two and we would assess the possibility of the incoming severe storm that was forecast. It looked like it missed us, so at 3 p.m. I set out on a 6.6-mile leg, and of course, the storm hit around thirty minutes into the hike. The good news was that the temperature dropped considerably and the bugs went away. If you can get over the sound of thunder, wet feet, and it being more slippery, it was fine. I had my jacket and just kept going.

At my next stop, I met another recent college graduate who was given the trail name "Pretty Boy." He has been also doing a lot of miles and has had support for the last few days. The common thread for many of these young people doing big miles is that they ran cross country in high school (go Lake Braddock!). I think they learn to suffer and keep going. I try to keep my level of intensity consistent when I hike. This is very different than I taught my girls in the past on the Burke Athletic Club (BAC) United soccer team—the best girls in the world (with the best parents in the world). In soccer, you want to vary your level of intensity throughout the game—bursts of speed and then slow. In endurance sports, you want to always keep at the same level. I have not been able to do that lately until today. The terrain today had long gradual ups and downs with few obstacles to slow me down. It was kind of the perfect storm today, with the weather and the bugs in check. Most of all, I think I was able to do more miles today because my family gave me so much energy from their visit on Father's Day. My feet did not even hurt at the end of the day (maybe the padding from the new socks).

Former BAC United Soccer Player (Caroline) yesterday.

4 Comments

Sue D

Whoop, whoop! Nothing better than family love. . . . And new socks! Congrats on one-third down. Go, Tommy, go!

Beatrix T

BAC United had the best coach in the world. Now we are cheering you on from the sidelines. Go coach Tom!

Steve H

Epic shot of you at McAfee Knob.

I thought of you as I ran Grandma's Marathon on the 18th. It went something like, "A marathon of hiking a day for 90 days is a lot of miles."

Keep up the great work and the entertaining posts!

Beatrix T

Burke United Soccer had the best coach in the world. We are cheering you on from the sidelines now. Go Coach Tom!

Cool Breeze and Blitz

Day 30: The day after

06/21/2017

Miles Hiked: 28.1

Total Miles: 795.2

Banked Miles: 66.1

It was a little harder hiking than usual today. I might have overdone it a tad yesterday. I got started at around 7 a.m. this morning and my legs felt like lead weights. I fought through it and made it to the James River Bridge by 12:45 p.m. I knew I had a big climb ahead of me, so I tried to eat and drink a lot before starting, and I took extra water with me up the mountain. It was so hard! Normally I do not mind climbing. A lot has to do with the heat, combined with the climb. When I got to the top, I was exhausted and had already made three stops to drink whereas I normally do not stop. It was then I met Blitz. He is a German hiker (software engineer) who also likes to hike big miles. He was trying to do thirty-four miles today. We hiked together the rest of the afternoon and it took our minds off how tired we were. When we got back to the van around 5:30, Mick had gotten me a Pepperoni and black olive pizza from Pizza Hut and a lemonade. I shared both with my new friend Blitz. It was all gone in about three seconds. I also introduced Blitz to his favorite new drink, Mountain Dew, and his new favorite chocolates, Baby Ruth and Butterfingers. We try to eat and drink healthy on the Trail. No thru-hiker ever seems to turn down Trail magic. Blitz then headed on to try to get to a shelter nine miles farther. Perhaps I will run into him again tomorrow. I lay down on my bed in the van and literally did not move for around two hours. I heard Mick outside talking to other hikers, but I just could not move. I am feeling more rested now. I have another big climb tomorrow. I think I will start earlier so I can get through it before it gets too hot.

My rattlesnake (look closely).

Day 31: My first rattlesnake

06/22/2017

Miles Hiked: 36.3

Total Miles: 831.5

Banked Miles: 78.1

Sorry this is late—did not have Internet last night. I got started at 6:15 a.m., but I was feeling quite down mentally as I walked. I didn't know why, but I knew I had to change something or it was going to be a long, long day. At my four mile break at Pedlar Gap (the 800-mile point on the AT), I ate two Krispy Kreme Donuts and two hard-boiled eggs and then a lot of water, a diet Mountain Dew, and lemonade. Mick was making tea and coffee for all the thru-hikers who had been camping there. He was very popular. I walked another six miles and got to the big climb I spoke about yesterday. It was not too hot yet and the terrain was smooth, so up I went. I was almost to the top when I heard a rattle. I thought, "There must be a rattlesnake around here." I looked around and then down to the ground and there it was. Its head was six inches from my low-cut trail running shoe with crew-length (short) socks. The Trail was around two feet wide. I do not know why I was to the right of it. Maybe I thought it was a stick and just avoided it. I had not seen it. Perhaps it is because I am colorblind and it just meshed with the environment. Anyway, I expeditiously moved forward a few feet (it was not coiled) and got my camera out to take a picture. I wish I was a better photographer. Then, around five minutes later, as I continued hiking at the top of the mountain, a little fawn (let's call him Bambi) came walking southbound down the trail. I stopped and tried to look friendly and it kept coming forward to within around ten feet of me. We stared at each other and I took pictures. Then, I had to continue, so I moved forward and Bambi gave way. I hope Bambi is not so trusting with Mr. Rattlesnake.

Sometimes the road crossings in the "book" are not accessible by car. This was the case at the end of my hike today. I was only planning thirty miles, but Mick could not get me at the last two crossings. I had to go an additional six miles (two hours). The terrain had been perfect all day, but when you are really tired, the Trail decides to get you. There was a one-mile big climb (no problem) followed by five miles of rocks going downhill. The pain from each oddly shaped, sharp rock rising from beneath the ground is magnified around three times when your feet are already tired and hurt. It was not a fun way to end the hike—more of a reminder that this is not easy. I arrived back at the van at 8 p.m. It was a long day of hiking.

3 Comments

Catherine L

Hi Tom, It's amazing how calmly you are dealing with all of those wildlife encounters! From the comfort of my home, it sounds quite unnerving. Bummer about the extra six miles today. Good news is at least you didn't get lost! You can bank it for another day. Have you thought about getting a thicker-soled shoe for the rocky terrain? PA will be worse. Also, I remember E got new boots every 700 or so miles. You are doing great! Love your posts. Xo, Cathy

Sue D

You're doing great, Tommy! Love the Bambi photo (hate the snake).

Uncle Ken

Way to go, Cool Breeze. Keep on keepin' on.

Great snake and fawn!

Cousin Mac, Cool Breeze, and Mick the Sherpa.

Day 32: Cousin Mac visits Cool Breeze

Miles Hiked: 29.8
Total Miles: 861.3
Banked Miles: 83.6

06/23/2017

I started today hiking again with Blitz. He had made his dinner in our van last night and tented nearby. My feet really hurt a lot all last night. Mick thinks it was that the van was parked leaning towards the front and the blood went to my feet. The first twenty miles of today's hike was then on a lot of rocks, which hurt my feet even more. This did not make me happy. My order of unpleasantness on the Trail is currently rocks, followed by gnats, flies and mosquitoes, followed by heat and humidity. Today, we had all three. However, talking with Blitz all morning was a good distraction, and Mick went to the Devil's Backbone Brewery to get us a lot of food for lunch. I had a big burger. The last ten miles today was smooth sailing, and we ended our hiking day on a high note. My cousin Mac lives in Charlottesville, VA. He and his family would always spend Christmas and Thanksgiving together with us. He now lives down here, less than an hour away, and his daughter Jody (around my age) and her family now live in NYC (she will hopefully visit me up there), so we do not see each other very much anymore. It was great seeing him and his friend Carol tonight. They were the first people to visit me other than my wife and kids. We had dinner at Applebees (like Ricky Bobby in Talladega Nights), and I ate a lot. We are now at the start of Skyline Drive. It is my plan to make a visit to Washington DC and my home on Sunday evening. I hope to be at Medium Rare Bethesda from 6–6:30; Medium Rare Cleveland Park for 7–7:30; and Medium Rare Barracks Row from 8–8:30—if anyone wants to stop by and say hello to me. . . .

Bear No.10

Day 33: Trump tweets about Cool Breeze

Miles Hiked: 28.1
Total Miles: 891.1
Banked Miles: 87.4

06/24/2017

Ok, Trump tweeting about me is fake news. What is real news is that I saw my tenth bear while hiking in Virginia today. This time, Mick was hiking with me. He had not seen a bear while hiking before. I was feeling relaxed and confident when I saw this bear as I knew, even after twenty-eight miles, I was still faster than Mick (right, Sue?). It did not run away right away. We were so close to a big public campground; I think it was more used to people.

I started hiking today around 7:30 a.m., which is pretty late for me, but I only had to hike twenty-five miles so I felt I could take my time. I developed a slight shin splint yesterday and it was a little worse today. I want to be very careful about it as I have had them in the past and they hurt. When you are taking five million steps, you do not want to feel pain on each step. Around ten years ago, my brother-in-law Dan showed me some good stretches to prevent shin splints. I have never had any problem with them since that time. So, I was surprised when I got that feeling yesterday. When you are hiking tired, you make some mistakes, and that is usually what causes injury. Anyway, I am going to be very careful the next day or two so it does not get any worse. The good thing today was that the Skyline Drive gave me very hiker friendly terrain. I could not complain about anything, except, one area did not have enough white blazes to follow, and I kept having to check my Guthook app to ensure I was still on the Trail as there are so many side trails for day hikers here. I briefly met two young ladies today thru-hiking the AT, and they were twins. I bet my twin nieces Anna and Eleanor (age seven) will hike the Trail together some day. They did two miles on the AT that I supported with Elisabeth last fall. I do not know if I mentioned this earlier, but I met a family hiking last week with twins (a boy and girl) who are now seven but hiked the entire AT with their parents at ages three and four. I am sure this is a record. I got to take a 5.25-minute shower tonight for $1.75 in quarters as we were required to park the van at the Loft Mountain Campground and they had showers (I walked the three extra miles to get to the campground). I am getting excited about visiting home on Sunday.

My breakfast choices.

Day 34: Shin Splints

Miles Hiked: 30.1
Total Miles: 921.2
Banked Miles: 93.2

06/25/2017

After my first four-mile leg this morning, I felt the shin splints in my left leg were worse rather than better. I decided to ice them during my breaks and take Advil. I will probably get a compression bandage also. The Advil seems to manage the pain so I can more easily walk. I also really slowed down to avoid any movements that could make it worse. I am pretty lucky that the last two days have been super hiker-friendly. There have been very few rocks to contend with that would put my feet in awkward positions, thus aggravating my shin. On the other hand, if my shin did not hurt, I would be getting finished hours quicker than normal or going farther. . . .

During my second leg of hiking, Mick went back to the campground restaurant and got me breakfast. It was strange that they were not open for breakfast until 9am. I got both an egg sandwich and pancakes. It was great. It is amazing what I can eat now and not feel guilty about it. I had a vanilla milkshake last night. I still do not have the "big" thru-hiker appetite, where they can eat everything on the menu. Skyline Drive was very busy today (Saturday), and we could not get a spot for the van at any of the campgrounds for the night; however, there were very few hikers I saw on the Trail. We do not have a signal again where we parked, so I will not be able to publish this until sometime tomorrow.

One Comment

Uncle Kevin
> Tom,
> You are doing awesome. I know you will approach your situation wisely to achieve your goal.

Skyline Drive view.

Day 35: A visit home

Miles Hiked: 20.2
Total Miles: 941.4
Banked Miles: 89.1

06/26/2017

I started right at 6 a.m. My goal was to hike twenty miles by 1 p.m. I knew right when I started that the shin splints were worse, leaving me with a limp. I had to hope that the Advil had not yet kicked in and I would be able to walk. A few minutes later, I was walking in a more normal fashion. Although Mick met me approximately every five miles, I took only one break at fifteen miles to change my socks. I finished a little later than I hoped, at 1:20, but good enough. It was quite rocky today on Skyline Drive, which was a change. As it was Sunday, the Trail got pretty crowded with day hikers by noon. I was very happy to take the afternoon off and excited to go home.

I got home a little after 3 p.m. and was very happy to see my wife and my daughter Caroline (and Cosmo). I was only able to stay a little while as I had to leave at 4:30 to go see my parents. Caroline went with me. My parents seemed happy to see me, and I think they enjoyed my stories. We then proceeded to all three Medium Rare's. It was great seeing everyone and eating the steak and fries (and secret sauce) again. Our staff is great at all locations. My daughter Sara and her friend Lydia were at the Cleveland Park location, which made it even more fun. My high school friend Rick was at our Capitol Hill location, and we got to talk while Caroline and I easily polished off a hot fudge sundae. We got home early enough that I got to spend some time with my wife before going to sleep in a real bed. Overall, it was great to come home.

Our dog, Cosmo.

3 Comments

Beatrix T

I wish I had read your previous couple days before today. Would have loved to visit with you. We continue to root for you from the sidelines. We very much enjoy reading your reports and we watch your progress with anticipation. Sometimes a few days late but we have not missed a day. Go Tom!

Sue D

Love this. Heartwarming! Hope you got some to-go steak, fries and secret sauce for your backpack!

Jennifer G

Aside from the shin splints, this sounds like a perfect day! Family, Friends, Fries, Fudge & Furry Boy.

Love you and Miss you lots,

Jennjenn

Me and two members of the Appalachian Trail Institute (ATI) expedition.

Day 36: Back on the Trail

06/27/2017

Miles Hiked: 30

Total Miles: 961.4

Banked Miles: 84.8

I did not get to sleep-in this morning as I had a meeting in Marshall, Va. at 8am. I have a monthly meeting with my Young President's Organization (YPO) forum group. We have eight people in our group and we pride ourselves in not missing a meeting—even if we are hiking the AT. My friend Jon has a farm in Marshall, and he was nice enough to host the meeting there so I could more quickly get on the Trail.

I got back on the Trail at 2 p.m. and I was determined to do twenty miles before dark. My shin splints made it hard to walk this morning. By this afternoon, my lower left leg was noticeably bigger than the right. It remained that way all afternoon as I walked. I took Advil only once, at 2 p.m., and finished my hike at 9 p.m.

As I only did partial days for the last two days, some of my hiking friends have caught up to me, and I got to hike with Pretty Boy for around five miles and also a guy named One Night Stand. I also heard Blitz is now in front of me, but I think he is only one mile ahead now. Bear number eleven was quite small, and around thirty yards away, walking on a log up the hill, not paying me any attention. I have run into Warren Doyle's ATI expedition (my Appalachian Trail Institute school), where a group of people all thru-hike together with van support—though it is one van for everyone. Bear number twelve, a few hours later, was a little bigger, walking through the woods, also around thirty yards away. I am now just seven miles from Front Royal. I think this little break to visit home and go to my meeting was really good for my morale.

Yogi Bear, Blitz, Tom (Double Fault), Cool Breeze, and Mick.

Day 37: A visit from Tom

06/28/2017

Miles Hiked: 27.7

Total Miles: 989.1

Banked Miles: 88.2

What a day. I walked around eight miles before meeting Mick, and we drove into Front Royal. Almost everyone I saw at home the other day thought I needed to eat more, so we went to the McDonalds drive-through and I got two sausage, egg, and cheese biscuit meals. After going to the post office to get Medium Rare mail, we went to the grocery store where I bought a myriad of unhealthy food items that I thought would have more calories, including donuts, cookies, and Twinkies. I then returned to the Trail feeling that I had added a few calories to my diet. A little farther up the Trail, I met-up with Blitz again. It was great seeing him. I ended up hiking with him and Yogi Bear (a twenty-one year-old hiker who will be returning to Hamilton College this fall). The time went very fast today hiking with two people. However, the big excitement was my friend Tom was also coming to see me on the Trail. Tom was the first of my friends brave enough to hike with me, and he did a great job. Aside from doing my insurance, Tom and I were formidable tennis partners for many years. We went by the Tom-Toms. He hiked in with Mick at Ashby Gap on Route 50 around four miles west of Upperville, Virginia. Tom had some shirts made for me at CustomInk, and he brought me some Dom champagne to celebrate with in the future. Wow! After we finished, we decided to go to one of my favorite pubs, which is in Upperville—the Hounds Head Tavern. There, my friends Stanislas and Maggie (who live nearby) also joined us. I had my first beer since I started the hike. It was a Guinness to go with my bangers and mash, as I need calories.

 I do not know if I have mentioned this, but Mick is a massage therapist by profession. I know, I know. Well, I have not used any of his message services until now. My lower left leg is now quite swollen. The shin splints do not really bother me on the Trail now, but it looks really bad. We wrapped it this afternoon (compression) and later in the evening Mick worked on me. It looked much better after he finished, but he warned me that the fluids in there would likely return.

Can you see the difference?

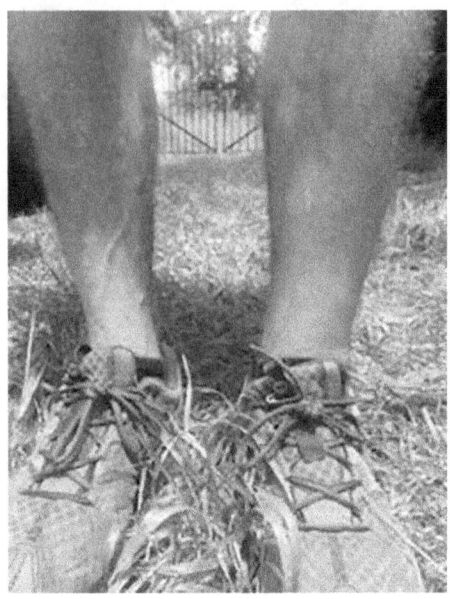

3 Comments

Catherine L

Wow! That does sound like a great day! I read somewhere that the "younger" hikers tend to have a big appetite and the "older" hikers don't which can lead to problems. You are wise to increase your daily caloric intake! Hoping your leg starts to feel better soon. Mick's treatments should help a lot. You are getting to close to the halfway point. . . . Amazing! Xo, Cathy

Alexandra D

Mick's a massage therapist?

The best burgers in Front Royal are at Spelunkers. Sounds like it was a fun day with friends. Miss ya!

Steve H

You will probably get as much fanfare as Scott Jurek did in 2015 when you reach the summit of Mt. Katahdin . . . he got a ticket for $500 for drinking in public in Baxter State Park. Keep the champagne spray to a minimum!

http://www.runnersworld.com/scott-jurek/scott-jurek-to-pay-500-fine-for-public-drinking-in-baxter-state-park

1,000 mile marker

Day 38: 1,000 Miles!

Miles Hiked: 27.7
Total Miles: 1016.8
Banked Miles: 91.6

06/29/2017

I did not start hiking until 8 a.m. as I had to attend to some Medium Rare business. It was around eleven miles before I reached the 1,000-mile point. It felt really good. However, today I had a relatively hard hike in an area known as the Roller Coaster. There were a lot of short up and downs, but mostly it was hard because of the rocks the entire way. I am still not going fast because of my little injury. I hiked this afternoon with a super nice young man from the Bronx who goes by the name Turbo (animated snail). I do not think he got the name because he hikes fast. Even he can keep up with me right now. He started the AT on March 30—almost two months before me. He stopped before me to go to something called a "hiker feed" where they would provide free dinners (local produce) to thru-hikers. I think most hikers were stopping there. I decided to continue another five miles. Mick met me a little after Turbo left and we walked together. At 7:20 p.m. we saw bear number thirteen on the Trail ahead of us. He ran down the Trail, away from us, when he saw us and then into the woods. At 7:45 p.m. we saw bear number fourteen in the woods. He was big. The biggest I have seen. He decided to just sit and watch us while we watched him. There were a good thirty yards and a lot of forest between us.

We are in West Virginia right now, literally between a sign that says Welcome to Virginia and a sign that says Welcome to West Virginia. We are also very close to Harpers Ferry. I think I will go to sleep early tonight.

Turbo and I.

ATC in Harpers Ferry with Blitz and Mick

Day 39: The fastest so far

Miles Hiked: 28.6
Total Miles: 1045.4
Banked Miles: 95.9

06/30/2017

I started at around 6:30 a.m., about six miles from historic Harpers Ferry. Harpers Ferry is almost at the half-way point of the Trail, and it is the home of the Appalachian Trail Conservancy (ATC) which is sort of the governing body of all things Appalachian Trail. Thru-hikers are supposed to stop there and check-in. They take your picture (this is a big deal for hikers) and you put information around it like start date and today's date and they put it in a big book. I was hiker number 1,161 to arrive this year going south to north. After putting my picture and information in the book, the volunteer working there and I paged through the book to see if anyone had gotten there faster than I. Nobody had so far. You do not have to stop there, so there may be some out there faster. I know there is a guy going for the record right now who was doing fifty-mile days (Crazy Knots), so he likely passed Harpers Ferry significantly faster than I. But for now, I am the fastest hiker who has checked-in at the ATC this year.

A volunteer also told me that there is a somewhat famous thru-hiker who also has the trail name Cool Breeze. This gentleman has hiked the AT four times. He then went and figured out all the best places to hike on the AT with the best cool breezes and this trail is supposedly on the AT website as a route you can do on the AT that they encourage people to do. I guess I do not mind being mistaken for this Cool Breeze.

Blitz made it to the ATC a little after I did. He and some other really good hikers (Phantom, Repeat, and Chipotle) are going to take the train in to visit DC today. They plan on eating at Medium Rare tonight. I hope they like it—I am pretty confident that Alex (our GM) at the Capitol Hill location will make sure it is memorable.

I said goodbye Virginia and West Virginia today and I said hello to Maryland (Boonsboro). Tomorrow, I will say goodbye to MD and say hello to PA. I will be in PA for a while. I saw a couple running down a hill at the end of the day saying to me I could go no further. There was a bear at the top of the hill. The woman was so scared that she had dropped her sunglasses and left them. I told them I think I would I would brave it and continue (they scared away my bear number fifteen which I was going to call Elisha Bear). I told them I would bring the sunglasses to the next road crossing, but they had had enough. Anyone want a pair of women's sunglasses?

One Comment

Angela T

Wow Tom you're doing great! To be the fastest thus far should be a great mental boost. These posts are great. When I miss a day I go back to catch up. Will you be putting all of your post together for a book in the end? Would be a inspiring and fun read.

LOL when I read your post, I envision the Cliff Hanger game on ThePrice Is Right. You humming the tune as you hike. You'll have to Google the tune. La da di do di do do do la di do do dooooo!

I think I need a shave.

Day 40: I'm in the North

07/01/2017

Miles Hiked: 37.6

Total Miles: 1083

Banked Miles: 109.2

Today I said goodbye to Maryland. I was born and raised in Potomac, MD. My parents still live in the same house where I grew up in. Many of my awesome childhood friends are reading this journal. I have many adult friends who now live in MD. The AT does not spend much time there, though. I reached the MD–PA border this morning. At the same place as the sign for the state borders, there was a sign indicating the Mason Dixon Line, putting me now in the north part of the US (so why is it still so hot and humid?). I have many good friends who are from Pennsylvania including Tom B and Henry K. My incredible in-laws Ellen and Ron currently live in PA. With the exception of their sports teams (and fans), PA is a pretty nice place. However, please do something about the rocks before I get to them—I am giving you plenty of time.

I decided to up my hiking pace as well as my mileage today (over thirty-seven miles). My shin is still swollen for some reason, but it really doesn't hurt. I am still being very cautious. I did a practice hike in this same area last fall, so I felt comfortable with the terrain, and we made a call at each road crossing whether or not to continue further. As I had been here before, I knew there was a hiker restaurant nearby where we finished at Caledonia State Park called Timbers. I had two large milkshakes at dinner tonight which I would never have had even one under normal circumstances. With the milkshakes, I had bacon cheese fries and a grilled cheese sandwich. Mick had bought me two Hardees cheeseburgers for lunch and I had one at each of two of my breaks. Timbers serves breakfast tomorrow; maybe an egg sandwich or pancakes or another milkshake? These are hard decisions for a thru-hiker.

My Journey through VA, WV, and MD

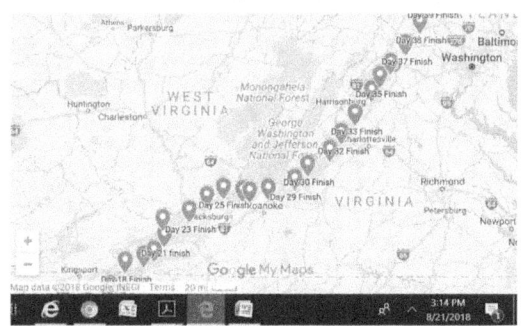

3 Comments

Uncle Kevin

Tom

Almost 38 miles in one day????? With shin splints???? You are a monster.

Welcome to the north, and congratulations to being just shy of half-way done.

In one day you hiked the equivalent of about one-quarter of the Northville–Placid Trail in the Adirondacks.

Jody

Hi Tom! You're making such great progress! My dad loved seeing you in Virginia but was concerned about your shins. So nice to go through Maryland—I have so many fond memories from there, as well. But up north you go, and I can't wait to see you in Warwick!

Love,

Jody

Alexandra D

You should use Four Square to check in when you're crossing all of these borders. I was the mayor of the Mason Dixon Line for a minute! Stay COOL!

The permanent 1/2 way sign.

Day 41: 1/2 Way!

Miles Hiked: 29.2
Total Miles: 1112.2
Banked Miles: 114.1

07/02/2017

How about that? I have done half of the Appalachian Trail in forty-one days (the toughest parts are in front of me). It was supposed to be one my favorite days. It was not. I started around 6:30 a.m. Mick and I seemed to be ready for that half-way talk to discuss the things that we do that gets on each other's nerves. I got finished my first few hours hoping he had gotten me something great for breakfast from the place we ate at last night, but instead there was lunch and another milkshake. I never specified what I wanted. Anyway, on the next stop I downed my third milkshake in less than twelve hours and Mick and I got ready to get the half-way photo. We walked for around two miles but could not find the half-way sign. We were clearly past the halfway point. I had hiked here last fall and had seen the sign. I was upset. I could not understand how we missed it. Did we get off the trail somehow and then get back on? I continued and met a lady who did not like the way I was hiking the trail and my stomach started to hurt from the excessive milkshake lactose. I kept thinking that I would have to go back as I missed the sign. Finally, I got to the main sign that does not move when the total AT mileage changes every year. I was sad Mick was not there, but I did a selfie in front of the sign. I then arrived at Pine Grove Furnace State Park. This is where the half-gallon challenge takes place. You are supposed to eat half a gallon of ice cream in one sitting when you arrive there. Unfortunately, the power was out because of the storms and the park store was closed. There were around twenty thru-hikers sitting outside hoping the power would return. Can you imagine if I ate a half-gallon of ice cream after three milkshakes? Perhaps this was a bit of luck for me. It turned out the moveable half-way sign was now right at the entrance of a road crossing behind a big Trail entrance sign. We just missed, it figuring it was on the Trail.

  I had around six miles to go in the day when I got to a junction and saw a white blaze and started heading down a dirt hill. I slipped backwards and did everything I could to avoid falling. This included really pointing my toes and digging in with them and my poles. I did not fall, but this really stretched my shin. It was not good. At the bottom of the hill I realized after looking at my Guthook map, I had gone the wrong way. Someone in PA paints side trails light blue instead of dark blue. It looks white to me as I am colorblind. As I was walking back up, I see Mick walking down. He is not colorblind and thought the blaze looked white also and went that way (at closer inspection he realized it was blue).

After returning to the van which was close by, I decided to break my remaining six miles into two three-mile legs. I took some Advil, wrapped my shin with a pressure bandage and put on my heavier hiking shoes I brought from home to help against the rocks. It was not good regarding the shin. It hurt more than it did when I originally injured it. I decided to shut it down after the first three miles. Mick spent some time working on my shin (and I iced it), but I am not sure what tomorrow will bring for the first time. Here is the drama that I promised you. . . .

2 Comments

Bobby

    Tom—Congrats on halfway—it makes me a little sad—I look forward to reading your posts everyday—don't want them to end.

    Bobby

Uncle Ken

    Congrats on the half-way mark! Awesome accomplishment.

    Hope you can tap into your bank reserve, moderate your pace, and care for that leg as the long term business strategy.

A harmless black snake on the Trail.

Day 42: A much better day

07/03/2017

Miles Hiked: 25.6

Total Miles: 1137.8

Banked Miles: 115.4

I decided to sleep in until 7 a.m. We then drove to a Cracker Barrel Restaurant in Carlyle, PA, for some breakfast. This gave my shin a little more recovery time and I could ice it some more, etc. As I do not want to hike in the dark, it also makes it harder for me to decide to keep going another six or seven miles at the end of the day. When I got started at 9:15 a.m., there were three thru-hikers sitting on the side of the road. I said I was nursing my shin and they told me I was about to go through the rock maze. They described it as a big boulder field where it is difficult to even know which way to go—so they had heard and read. I try not to listen to this stuff as it is usually poor information, but I worried my shin would be tested immediately. The rock maze was a maze. If you followed it, you did not have to go over practically any rocks. This was followed by eighteen miles of flat and smooth terrain in the Cumberland Valley, walking through farms and cute towns like Boiling Springs (we have never been out of the mountains like this before). It was a perfect day not to have to test my shin. I think I was very lucky. I throttled down the pace again as well as the mileage.

It was actually kind of amazing. Last night I could not put any weight on my left leg going downhill and today it felt OK. It is hard to explain, but I felt like an athlete last night and today. I got done with my walk last night and immediately I started working with my trainer (Mick) doing everything we could do so I could perform the next day. We were a team. I like watching sports documentaries like *Dare to Dream*, *Meru*, *Running the Sahara*, and *Diana Nyad*, and they all had a team behind them and had to "walk through" injuries to be successful. My leg is still swollen and it hurts, but I definitely could continue the way it felt today. I think it is important to know the difference between pain and a serious injury that could really get worse. As I have experience with shin splints, and know that many AT hikers walk with them, it helps me to make the right decisions (so far—I think). We use to think concussions were just pain and not serious injuries that we had to recover from. Today, the heat and the gnats and flies were actually my biggest concerns, but I was very careful with my leg. Tomorrow, it is going to get much harder. . . .

3 Comments

Kate D

I'm glad you're feeling better, Tom! We saw Lish last night at Jay and Marcie's, and your shin splints were a big topic of conversation. We're all pulling for you, and hope your leg recovers soon. Congratulations on hitting the half-way point so quickly—your stamina and determination are truly inspiring. XOXO Katie

Jody

Hi Tom! Half-way must feel good, and I know that you are going to "rock" the rest of it.

Love,

Jody

Sue D

You're really moving! Here's to smooth terrain and cute towns. No more swollen shins and no more snakes!!!

View in Pennsylvania.

Day 43: Not too bad, yet

Miles Hiked: 26.5
Total Miles: 1164.3
Banked Miles: 117.6

07/04/2017

My leg felt good today. I did not have any pain today and the swelling is way down. I attribute this quick recovery to my trainer, Mick. So, I still need something to complain about. Today was the first day of the 150 miles of rocks. I still had fifteen miles to hike through Duncannon, PA where the rocks were to begin. As you remember, my big three complaints are rocks, bugs, and heat. I have been very worried about this rock section. Interestingly, I had no issues with the rocks today. There were big, smooth boulders I could hop across or smaller rocks that still had places around them to put my foot, so I did not need to always step on them. Most of the way today was pretty smooth trail—granted I am only 10 percent in the rock section, so not a big sample size. It was hot today, but not too bad. The bugs were awful. More specifically, the gnats (not the Nats – go Nats!). They were pervasive, constant, and relentless. Basically, they were driving me crazy. It is hard to walk over or between rocks while swatting at the gnats from your ears with your hand or trekking pole. I have tried every bug spray from Vanilla to Citronella to Deep Woods Off to Deet—nothing works. I could wear a mosquito net but it messes with my vision, is hot, and makes me look like a dork (OK, I am already a dork.). Around 3 p.m., I figured out how to pull down material from inside my ball cap over my ears. It was a game changer. The buzzing sound immediately stopped. The swatting was reduced by 75 percent. I now only had to swat the gnats from my face. Tomorrow, I will also wear my sunglasses (I have not worn them once on the Trail as we are always under the green forest canopy). Growing up in Potomac, I remember how bad the gnats were. Our moms would have to remove many from our eyes with their fingernails. The worst was when they went down your ear canal—it was painful. You would have to lie on your side so the gnat would climb up and then they would shine a flashlight at your ear to get them to come to the light. It's funny, the bugs don't bother some people at all. The rocks don't bother other people. Certain hikers do not mind the heat. However, they have other things that bother them that don't bother me—like the rain.

When we got back to the car, Iceman and his wife Barb had decided to provide a picnic for the hikers (Trail magic) at the exact location we were finishing (by a beautiful stream). Iceman had recently finished hiking the entire AT over six years. They cooked hamburgers and hot dogs, and they had watermelon, chips, soda, and cake. It was great. We had made some friends during the day including Sandals, Good Witch, and Lanky who were also there. There were probably a total of ten thru-hikers that we got to sit and chat with. It was one of my favorite nights on the Trail.

2 Comments

Rob Doo

Keep chugging, Tom. Go easy on the rocks.

Rob

Steve H

Gnats can be so bad. Good call on the ear flaps.

The photos on the web page are great. Except I wish they had a larger version you could open to see better!

Cool Breeze and Sandals.

Day 44: Happy 4th of July

07/05/2017

Miles Hiked: 28.8

Total Miles: 1193.1

Banked Miles: 122.1

I started at 6:15 a.m. on a 15.4-mile leg. My new friend Sandals said he might come with me, but he wasn't awake/there when I got going. Around 2.5 hours into the hike, here he comes from behind. He had started at 7am and had caught me. He must have been flying. We hiked the rest of the day together and talked. He is a really nice 20 year old young man from South Carolina who hopes to get into missionary work in the future. The funny thing is that I asked him at around lunch time if he had met any girls he liked on the Trail. He started talking about this one girl who was so nice who was going southbound. After a few minutes I said, "That's my niece, Elisabeth." He was mortified. It is a small world on the Trail. Anyway, another really good day hiking with Sandals (he has worn his sandals the entire way). The gnats were even worse today. Hikers are all starting to get out bug nets. The sunglasses make things better, but there are so many of them. I kept thinking about sci-fi movies and that the gnats were learning as I walked and soon they would know how to get under my glasses and under my hat.

I met bear number 15 today, and decided to name it Elisha Bear, after my wife, because it was so cute (and intelligent). It did not run away as I approached; it was simply late for an appointment. This was my first non-Virginia bear. In the evening, we walked from the van near Pine Grove, PA, to an overlook we had passed on the Trail just a couple hundred yards away to watch the fireworks. It was quite crowded with a big group of thru-hikers (a few intoxicated). We could see many firework displays in the valley below, but we were so high above them they looked like they were just a few feet off the ground. The rocks were again not too bad.

3 Comments

Alexandra D
> All right . . . I can read the miles . . . HOW MANY HAVE YOU DONE? Looks like 11 thousand.

Uncle Ken
> So, where is the picture of this cute, intelligent, and late Elisha Bear?

Kate Desvenain
> Home Remedy Gnat Repellant:

Ingredients

1/3 cup imitation vanilla

1/3 regular Listerine mouthwash

1/3 water

1 small, plastic spray bottle

Couldn't hurt to try! XOXO Kate

Soaking feet in hot water and Tiger Balm after the rocks.

Day 45: Ah oui, the rocks

Miles Hiked: 30.1
Total Miles: 1223.1
Banked Miles: 127.9

07/06/2017

OK, today we had rocks. We had a lot of rocks. To paint a picture, it is still a trail, but I would say one-third is still dirt and relatively smooth, one-third had either big boulders on which you could hop from one to the other or rocks that were separated enough to still find places to put your foot on the dirt, and one-third of the way was the little, sharp, jagged rocks of different shapes and sizes that protrude from dirt and are so prevalent that you are forced to step on them. The final third is what I do not like. None of this is really difficult. Any of you could walk any of this with no problem, but after a mile, you would probably have had enough of it. After thirty miles today, the meat on my feet was well tenderized. It was actually a lot better than I imagined: I imagined the entire thirty miles to be the little, jagged rocks, not just 10 miles. However, the beginning of the day was harder because of my gnat friends. While I was hiking, I asked Mick to buy me head (bug) netting. I learned that every time I swatted at the gnats in front of my face, I had four seconds until they all regrouped and came back. So, I got into a four-count rhythm on which the last beat was a window wiping movement in front of my face with my left trekking pole and then another four-count and I wiped with my right pole. It was the best I could do. Then, at around 2 p.m., there were no more gnats. It was as if the game people from the *Hunger Games* movie decided I did not need them anymore, as the rocks were now hard enough, so they turned them off. I hope they do not come back.

We are now very close to the town of Hamburg, PA. We found a nice pizza place after I stopped hiking. Tomorrow is more rocks. I think the *Hunger Games* people are going to introduce a lot of rain and the slippery rock factor. My shin feels really good right now, but each time I step on a rock and the rock "rocks" forward or backwards, I am reminded that it is still healing and I need to be careful (after a few choice words come from my mouth).

Why am I smiling?

Day 46: Slippery Rock

Miles Hiked: 25.2
Total Miles: 1248.4
Banked Miles: 128.8

07/07/2017

OMG, this was the hardest day for me on the Trail so far. On the one hand, it was raining, so it was cool and there were few gnats about which I could complain. There were hardly any big ups and downs. However, there were rocks—endless rocks. On top of that, the rocks were slippery (good name for a college, Craig?). Yesterday I talked about hopping over rocks in the boulder fields. Today, it was not possible for me. In fact, I started wishing I had more of the little jagged rocks (maybe I could just think of them as a deep tissue massage). I walked one nine-mile stretch in four hours. Usually, I walk twelve miles in four hours. When I was done with that stretch, my feet and legs were totally wiped out, but it was only 11 a.m.

I got a call from my business partner Steve in the afternoon with a question about Verizon while I was struggling in this huge boulder field with rocks as far as I could see in front of me and behind me (can you hear me now?). I felt like Walter Mitty in the movie, standing on a mountain in the Himalayas when the E-Harmony guy calls him to chat about his dating status.

At around 3 p.m., I decided twenty-five miles was all I could do today. My last leg was five miles. Mick had gotten me a vanilla milkshake and some chicken, so I was re-energized to knock this last part out. One of the things that had been bothering me during the day was that my ATI school notes said that this last stretch had the hard rocks. What? What had I been walking on all day? I get around three miles in and I am feeling good when I see two tents with hikers in them (6 p.m.). I said hello and a quick conversation ensued and the man let me know that I was six-tenths of a mile from the Knife's Edge, making a pyramid shape with his hands. He said he was told it should not be attempted when wet, so they were waiting until tomorrow. Great. Mick was waiting for me two miles ahead. I powered ahead so as not to have time to worry too much. When I got there, it was just as described—around one-hundred yards of what looked to me like a steep roofline with shingles. I had no choice but to continue. I was alone, as nobody else was stupid enough to be doing it, I guess. As I have mentioned, I am very afraid of heights. I realized immediately that I would not be able to stand much, as my feet slipped when I did. So, I made much of the way across on my butt. I do not know how long it took me, nor did I even think of taking a picture. However, I did feel a sense of accomplishment when I got through it, even if I did it mostly on my rear end.

Climbing Lehigh Gap.

Day 47: Not my finest hour

Miles Hiked: 21
Total Miles: 1269.4
Banked Miles: 125.8

07/08/2017

This morning was probably my low point on the Trail. It was pouring rain when I awoke. I decided to wait. At 9 a.m. it was still raining and I did not know when it would stop so I thought I would do three miles and see how it went. Well, it was awful. It took me two hours to get three miles. At one point I lowered myself down a rock cliff (again on my butt) only to find no white blazes to follow. This was not a good experience which I do not even want to talk about. . . . I felt totally defeated when I finally arrived at the van, all banged-up. This is all with the knowledge in the back of my head that five miles up ahead was Lehigh Gap—the one place on the entire AT that my friend Kit (Don't Matter) said I might have fear of heights issues.

Luckily, the next five miles were easy and the rain stopped. I arrived at the bottom of Lehigh Gap and there was a couple who had set-up a table with all sorts of Trail magic (sandwiches, drinks, watermelon, etc.) and they invited me to sit and enjoy. I asked Mick to climb the exposed, sheer rock face with me in case I panicked. I had so little confidence in myself after the last two days. The whole time going up this one mile climb, I kept thinking what it would be like if it was still raining and the rocks were wet. I would probably have tried to do it, but I would have really regretted it. This climb actually required using your hands and feet pulling you up in places (thanks for the lessons at the rock climbing place, Caroline). Mick helped me a lot getting through it. In the end, I think it was less a heights thing and more a, "if I slip and fall, it will not be good" thing. I tried to think of the day as an accomplishment, but I cannot right now.

The rest of the day was much easier for me. It is like night and day when the rocks are dry. I could again hop over them rather than trying to find footholds between them. I left at 9 a.m. and finished at 7 p.m. and only did twenty-one miles. It is not supposed to rain for the next two days, which should get me beyond the rocks. Hopefully, my confidence will start to return tomorrow.

Not fun for me

3 Comments

Sue D

You're doing great, Tommy! Every day is one step closer. We are all pulling for you and watching in awe!

Alexandra D

Keep trucking along! You'll be fine. Just imagine we are all late for a meeting . . . that should fuel your gusto to get through. Miss ya!

Uncle Ken

Way to go, Tom. Great accomplishment knowing you can get through those tough spots. It's hard work, but have fun.

Never thought I would be so happy coming to New Jersey.

Day 48: Rocks be damned

07/09/2017

Miles Hiked: 34.1

Total Miles: 1303.5

Banked Miles: 135.6

I decided to stop complaining, put my head down, increase my pace, and power through the rocks of Pennsylvania today. At around 4:30 p.m., I said goodbye to PA. In the words of the most famous person in the history of the state (more than the real Ben Franklin), Rocky, after Apollo Creed said, "Ain't gonna be no rematch." Rocky said, "Don't want one." That's all I am going to say about that.

I talked to my brother John last night and convinced him to come pay me a visit today. He lives in Princeton, NJ, so it was around a 1.5-hour drive. He, Mick, and I had a nice dinner at the Buck Hill Brewery in Blairsville, NJ. I am pretty tired now, so we will return to the trailhead at the Mohican Outdoor Center to stay for the night in the van.

One Comment

Karen S

You are doing great Tom. I have been enjoying the posts and your pictures. Sorry to hear the gnats are so bad. What a journey!

Uncle Ken and Aunt Martha with me and Mick at Trail Magic dinner.

Day 49: Great day in NJ

07/10/2017

Miles Hiked: 26.9

Total Miles: 1330.4

Banked Miles: 138.2

New Jersey has been great. When I think of Jersey, I still think of the Joe Piscopo character from SNL saying, "Are you from Jersey? I'm from Jersey." He was wearing a hard hat in front of a chemical plant eating a sandwich wondering why the food always tasted better as the chemicals spilled from the hat onto his sandwich. These big, ugly processing plants are the view of Jersey I get from the car or train every time I go to NYC. However, this is not the New Jersey I see while walking the AT. It is one of the more beautiful walks I have had on the Trail. It is such a far cry from Pennsylvania. I had my head up today, enjoying the hike.

The best part of the day was when my wife's Uncle Ken and Aunt Martha arrived for a visit. My wife has the best family! I will talk about all of them more soon. Ken and Martha hiked into me with Mick and we all walked back out together. Then, Ken hiked with me another four miles while Mick and Martha drove the vehicles forward and they again hiked into us and back out with us. When we got to the parking area, a group of super-nice people had set up (for two days) an unbelievable Trail magic spread that they invited all of us to partake of. We had drinks, hamburgers, sausages, hot dogs, almond cake, and this goes on and on. We all sat and talked outside in perfect evening weather. What a great end to the day. It was so great of Ken and Martha to visit me, and I had a great time today all around.

Our NJ Trail Angels!

One Comment

Amy D

Thank you for your kind words, Cool Breeze! It was great meeting you! Best of luck for a safe hike. We look forward to following your journey all the way to Katahdin. Hike on!

Love, the "NJ Grillers"

Scallywag and I on the Boadwalk

Day 50: I met a Scallywag

Miles Hiked: 31.4
Total Miles: 1361.8
Banked Miles: 145.3

07/11/2017

Again, I have had a great time in New Jersey. I started hiking at 6 a.m. and finished around 7 p.m. Mick had gotten me an omelet for breakfast, a burger for lunch, and an ice cream snack, and they were great There was another person serving Trail magic breakfast to everyone passing by this morning, but I was set. It has amazed me how much Trail magic there has been the last week or so. I met and hiked with a very accomplished hiker this afternoon that goes by Scallywag. He is completing the triple crown of US distance hiking. He has already completed the Pacific Crest Trail (PCT) and the Continental Divide Trail (CDT) and now he is finishing the AT. He was very nice and it was fun listening to his stories. We hiked over nine-tenths of a mile of wooden planks called the Boardwalk (not exactly like at Ocean City) and then I hiked-up Stairway to Heaven. I am right at the NJ/NY border, near Warwick, NY.

I always talk about what I did during the day in the journal, but I rarely talk about what I was thinking while I walk each day—ten hours, plus or minus—usually by myself. Well, I think about all of you who are friends and family. I wanted to start writing a little about the people whom I thought about that day and who have positively influenced my life (you). Today I thought a lot about my Aunt Nancy (my father's sister). It was her birthday yesterday. I will not tell you how old she is as that would not be right (seventy). I have always wanted to be like my Aunt Nancy. A boy of my generation wanting to be like someone who is female was probably not very common. When I was five years old, I already wanted to go to the University of Colorado because that is where she went. When I was in sixth grade, I begged and got my parents to let me go live with her in Aspen for a few months to learn to ski. My Aunt was the head tennis pro at Snowmass Country Club at the time. She had just met my future Uncle Roger. Anyone who could survive me was a keeper. My Aunt is so sweet and nice as she beats you in anything she plays. You could lose to her in tennis 6-0, 6-0, and she would make you feel good about your game. We really bonded back then. We only got in one argument when she threw my skis out of the car for my comments about her green spaghetti. Whenever we spend time together, I never stop laughing. It is always one fun competition after the other. When we play tennis, we think so much alike it is scary. My Aunt is still a seriously competitive tennis player and golfer (former pro in each sport) and a champion duplicate bridge player. They now live on an extensive horse and cattle ranch in Ocala, Florida, where she is also a horse whisperer with her horse Cheyenne. I still want to be just like my Aunt Nancy when I grow up.

One Comment

Steve H

Maybe a pair of climbing approach shoes would be helpful for the wet rock days. They have some of the grippy climbing rubber on them. I had a couple of pairs of the 5.10 Guide shoes and they were pretty sweet.

http://www.fiveten.com/us/closeouts/outdoor/guide-tennie-red

The spongy rubber on a pair of broomball shoes (yes, it is a MN thing) would grip the rocks like velcro, but they would not be very good for hiking!

https://www.dickssportinggoods.com/p/acacia-sports-grip-inator-broomball-shoes-16as2ugrpntrbrmblhka/16as2ugrpntrbrmblhka?camp=CSE:DSG_pg22441_ecom_PLA_452&gclid=Cj0KEQjwkZfLBRCzg-69tJy84N8BEiQAf-fAwql8n8Vx9Vvoz5oW0AUYm6Af_zEgomswlQklPcBhDgW8aAiAk8P8HAQ

Prospect Rock in New York.

Day 51: Welcome to NY

07/12/2017

Miles Hiked: 21.9

Total Miles: 1383.7

Banked Miles: 142.9

Today was a very difficult hiking day. I felt like I was back in Pennsylvania. We had a huge downpour at around 5 a.m. It was so bad that the rain started seeping through the seal of the window of the van on Mick's side, drenching his bed. As I knew there would be a lot of boulder climbs today, I decided not to leave too early. Unfortunately, I did not wait long enough. I left at 7:15 a.m. on a ten-mile leg and the Trail was not dry. More specifically, the rocks were wet. My shoes slipped on so many of the rocks, making walking difficult. I had only fallen four times so far in fifty days, and I fell twice this morning, with a myriad of close calls. I should not have been out there—lesson learned. Although it may be operator error, I am going to have to buy new shoes that have more traction. I am also going to have to use my banked miles when it rains and I am in rocky areas.

As the day continued, the rocks started to dry, but the climbs started getting harder. It was really more like rock climbing than hiking today. My poles were superfluous on so many sections as I had to pull myself up with my hands. I kept thinking there was no way I could have done these sections if the rocks had still been wet. In the end, I hiked only around twenty-two miles when I had planned to hike thirty miles. I was so tired and it was so hard for me. Luckily, my friend Jeff, who is the President of Guest Services, invited us to stay at the Bear Mountain Inn, which his company runs (along with many other properties). It was just what I needed after the hike today. Jeff and I used to play tennis and golf together (he is much better than I) and we were on the Board of the Starlight Children's Foundation. He probably has no idea how perfect this was for me. The hospitality of the Inn was outstanding. Mick and I met a lovely couple at dinner at the Inn that was very interested in doing a supported AT thru-hike. They were leaving a teaching post at West Point tomorrow for a little vacation before their new Army assignment in Germany. I wish them both all the luck. I saw my sixteenth bear today on the trail. I will name this one Jeff the Bear. I am told this one lives near a shelter near where I was, and it is supposedly brazen enough to steal people's food during the day with them sitting right there.

One Comment

Jeff M

I am glad that you guys enjoyed the nights rest. I wish that I could have made it out there with you. You are my hero!

A little bridge walk.

Day 52: Back to Bear Mountain

Miles Hiked: 25.3
Total Miles: 1409
Banked Miles: 143.9

07/13/2017

Although we drove to and stayed at the Bear Mountain Inn last night, we still had eighteen miles to hike to get to the Inn. As we were going to finish close by (and the Inn is so nice), we decided to stay at the Inn for a second night. The first five miles this morning made me think it would be a long day again with rocks, bad biting bugs, heat and humidity (100 percent). However, after Mick dowsed me with Deep Woods Off at our first break and the terrain started to get less rocky on the next ten miles, I knew it was going to be a better day. I hiked into Bear Mountain Inn around 1:30 for lunch. There were a lot of steep climbs but it was not rock climbing like yesterday, so I was happy about that. At the end of the day, the humidity kept me from wanting to do thirty-plus miles, but I was satisfied. When I was done, we went back to the Inn and I got to take a shower for the second day in a row. I had some paperwork that I needed to do today, so a nice desk in my room was a big help. It did not rain, so I was happy. I did not have to shut down my hike even earlier because of the slippery rocks.

One Comment

Sue D

Wow! So cool to track you on your hiking map—great progress! It looks like you're now sprinting from state to state. Love that you got to take two showers in a row. It's the little things. Go, Tommy, go!

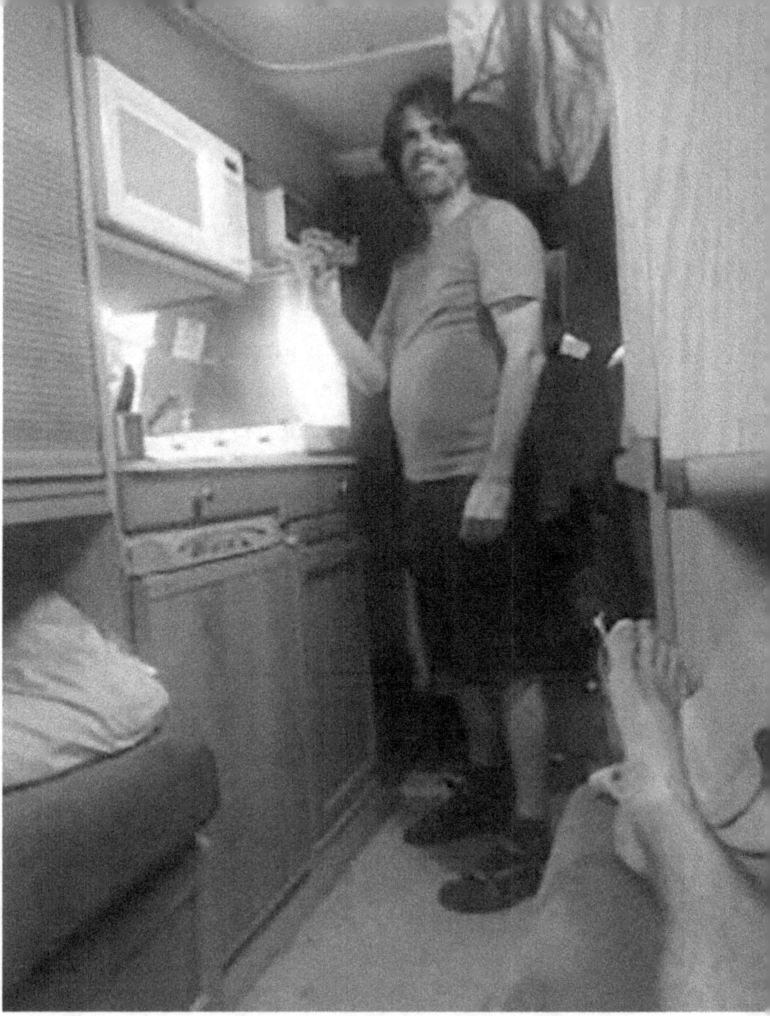

Mick staying cool in the van today.

Day 53: Hot and Humid

Miles Hiked: 31.4

Total Miles: 1440.4

Banked Miles: 151

07/14/2017

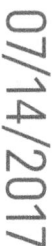

The good news was that the terrain was far easier today than past days. The lead story today was the heat and humidity—even when I started at 7 a.m. It does not outwardly bother me so much, like the bugs and the rocks, but it zaps my energy, making it near impossible to keep my normal pace. We really needed a cool breeze! Mick did not hike in to me today. I wonder why. Around 3 p.m. the clouds started to move in over me. As there were no big rocks to walk over today, I welcomed it. There was around an hour of thunder and light drizzle. At 4 p.m., the rain really came down. It was great. I was already wet all day from sweat, so this was the perfect shower and cool down. The rest of the day felt good, although I was pretty tired when I stopped at 8pm.

I was thinking about the neighborhood where I grew up, in Potomac, MD, today as I hiked. There were many positive influences that helped to shape me, but there were two people in particular from my neighborhood that I thought about—Mrs. Darling and Mr. Thane.

There were five kids in the Darling family. They lived two houses down from me. Robbie was my best friend (there is also Linda, Gary, Sue, and Sally—you see their comments sometimes in this journal). Mrs. Darling always made sure that I felt welcome when I came to their house, which was often. She always said that she wanted to adopt me. I think that this gave me a lot of confidence in life. It made me feel good every time she said it. Mrs. Darling always wanted to give me a kiss, but I refused to let her. She said I would have to let her kiss me on my wedding day, and I agreed, as I thought that day would never come. I have some great pictures from my wedding of Mrs. Darling giving me a kiss. She is not moving around so well right now, but I want Mrs. Darling to know that she is hiking with me every day in my thoughts.

There were four kids in the Thane family. They lived across the street from me. Linda was my age and my good friend (there is also Fritz, Trish, and Frank). I think the late Mrs. Thane would have also adopted me—she was an awesome person. Mr. Thane has always been such a good role model for me on how to live a good life and be a good person. My family could not screw in a light bulb. To this day he still helps my parents when something goes wrong in their house. He is in his nineties. He tried to teach me how to fix things when I was young, but I had no aptitude.

Mr. Thane would also give me advice on how to be a good person. For example, when I went to live in China, he thought it important to make sure I understood that I represented this country and our values. I always listened to what he told me because I always had such a huge respect for him as a person. As I mentioned, he is now in his nineties, and I think, if he wanted to, he could be the oldest person to thru-hike the AT.

2 Comments

Sue D

> Love this! I'm going to read it to our mom. She's been following your progress and I guarantee she's going to want to kiss you again when you finish the hike!

Rob D

> I often think back to the neighborhood and growing up with you and the other families. What a bunch of good people that positively influenced so many children.
>
> Some of you following may be interested to know that Tommy, while growing up, only ate American cheese on white bread sandwiches.
>
> Keep on Truckin'!

Cathy, Elisabeth, and Courtney join us on the AT.

Day 54: 2/3 of the way

07/15/2017

Miles Hiked: 26.3

Total Miles: 1466.7

Banked Miles: 153

The day started off great. It was raining and a cool 60 degrees with no humidity or bugs. The terrain had been easy for the last two days, with few rocks, and I expected it to continue. Then it happened. . . . At 11:30 a.m. my wife's sister Cathy arrived with her daughters Elisabeth (the thru-hiker) and Courtney (a recent high school honors graduate), and my day got ten times better. We had lunch at a nearby diner (milkshakes and burgers) and then Cathy and Courtney did a little hiking with me on the Trail as we crossed into Connecticut, which is where they live, while Mick and Elisabeth waited for us at the next road crossing. Courtney fixed an iPhone issue for me on the Trail in literally less than 1 second that I have been trying to figure out for days. Cathy also brought us a ton of good food and drink. I am eating French bread and brie while I write this.

They could not stay too long because they are celebrating Elisabeth's twentieth birthday tonight (Happy birthday, Elisabeth!). Well, I have decided that New York came in like a bear and out like a lamb. The best part was my stay at the Bear Mountain Inn—thanks, Jeff. Connecticut looked like a lamb until my last seven miles today. I was back into the rocks, and as it was raining, so they were wet rocks again. It took me the time I would normally hike ten miles to hike the seven miles. We immediately got in the van and headed into Kent, CT to go to an outfitter to get me some new shoes. I have decided that all three pairs that I have are worn out. Each has gone around five hundred to six hundred miles, including my prep prior to the start. I am getting shoes with better traction this time. My friend and fellow former BAC soccer coach Steve H. has been giving me some good advice. Unfortunately, the store that has trail shoes was closed, so I will have to try again in the morning. I only have one third of the AT to go. It seems to keep getting harder for me every day. Good thing I am saving so much in my banked miles. I have around six days saved so far.

Cathy and Cool Breeze in Connecticut.

One Comment

Uncle Ken

Congrats on another milestone. It was great walking with you a bit last weekend. We will be thinking about you at our family reunion on Saturday.

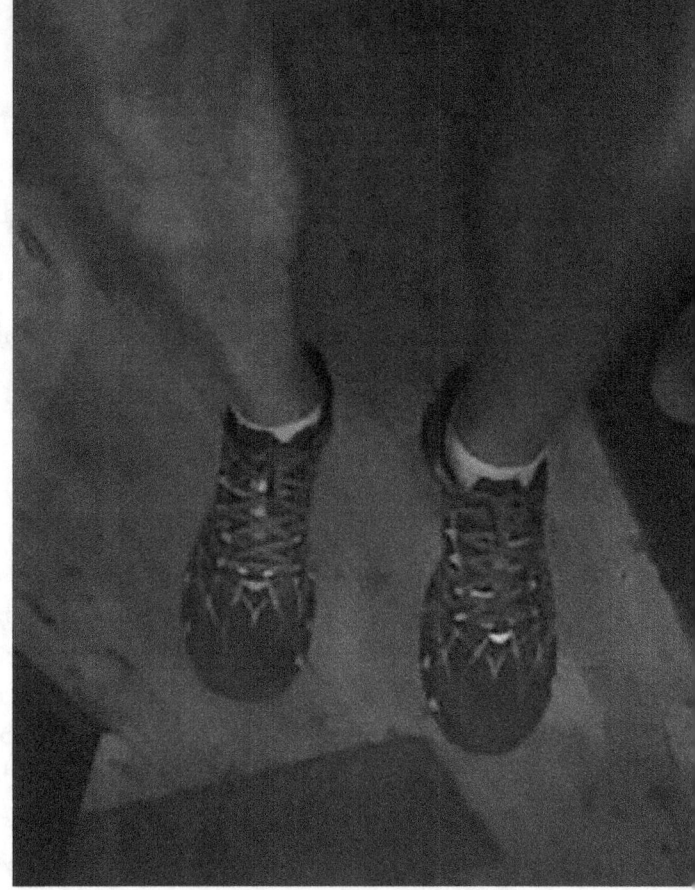

My new hiking kicks.

Day 55: New shoes

Miles Hiked: 25.6
Total Miles: 1492.3
Banked Miles: 154.3

07/16/2017

The rain woke me up around 5 a.m., which solidified my decision to get new shoes before I started hiking again. The problem was that the store that sold trail shoes did not open until 10 a.m. So, I went back to sleep for a while. We went into Kent around 8:30 and did some chores until 10 when the store opened. There were not too many choices. He only carried the shoes that the thru-hikers were specifically asking for. I tried on a few and chose a different pair of Merrill trail runners called Agility. They provided me a lot more cushion and comfort than my current shoes, but in the end, they did not offer more traction. I need to get another pair anyway to get me through the hike, so the next pair will need to offer more traction for the wet rocks. The problem is that I have to try them on, so I need to be in a place that offers a bigger variety and I have to come off the Trail to try them. When I finally got on the Trail this morning at 10:45 a.m., I immediately met a young man named Candles, and we walked together most of the day. He is twenty-four now, but I think in the future you will be reading the *New York Times Magazine* and there will an article about a really successful man, and in the article he will mention hiking the AT and his Trail name was Candles.

Today was my wife's family's annual family reunion in Pennsylvania. I am really sorry that I had to miss it this year. My wife's late father had five brothers and they are all married with children and grandchildren. My wife's family are all amazingly good people. I know how lucky I am to be a part of her family. Going to the reunion each year is a great experience. Usually, there are several new doctors or lawyers or engineers and new babies to get to know. If there was a Nobel Prize winner, the person would probably not mention it, as they are not boastful like me. However, they still seem to like me and include me. It is always a little hard as my wife's wonderful grandparents and Great Aunt Eleanor are no longer with us, but I believe they are responsible for how good their children and grandchildren turned out. I believe that I am a better person by getting to be part of her family. I will do my best to be there next year.

Candles and I in Connecticut.

One Comment

Jeff J

Tom, I just shot you an email and then remembered you are on your hike. Congrats on hitting Vermont. We will salute you tonight from Medium Rare on Capitol Hill.

Day 56: Welcome to Massachusetts

07/17/2017

Miles Hiked: 31.2
Total Miles: 1523.5
Banked Miles: 161.2

Today was a real mixed day for me. On the positive side, I walked over thirty miles; I made it to Massachusetts, and I met some interesting people at the end of the day. On the negative side, I have been having some real self doubt about my ability to do the 226 miles of really difficult mountains in New Hampshire and Maine. I have been having a lot of trouble making it up and down the steep rock sections that are being presented to me more and more the last few days. My supported strategy requires me to go a certain distance in a certain amount of time. When I get to the rocks, I move at around two miles an hour (or maybe less) and the math just doesn't work. This doesn't even take into account my fear of heights, the fact that I will likely be by myself, and the weather. If the rocks are wet, I can barely make any progress. I am going to really re-think my plan.

I said goodbye to Connecticut. It was a real mix of hard and not-so-hard areas with some very pretty views. The best part of Connecticut was the visit from Cathy, Elisabeth, and Courtney.

A day after my wife's family reunion, I thought a lot about my in-laws today, Ellen and Ron. No, they do not remind me of the difficult rocks. I know they have been hosting my wife and kids, Cathy's family, and my wife's brother Dan's family. There are a lot of people having a great time in one house on a little lake in Pennsylvania. Many people do not get along with their in-laws. I have had the opposite experience. I really like when they come to visit and I really enjoy visiting them. It feels so comfortable. I have given Ellen the honorary Trail name Grandma Smithwood, after Grandma Gatewood, the first woman to thru-hike the Appalachian Trail. Grandma Gatewood was sixty-seven years old at the time and a mother of thirteen. Grandma Smithwood not only followed Elisabeth's hike and my hike, but she also follows other random people's hikes on Trailjournals.com. She and I got along from the very first time we met, when I rented the movies *Throw Mama from the Train* and *I Think I Married An Ax Murderer*. When Ron and Grandma Smithwood lived in England, she would lead country walks through the UK. I hope I get to see them sometime on the Trail, but I am going so fast that I zipped right past them last week. This is another downside to my endurance-hiking strategy.

2 Comments

JR R

Tom, Take all that self-doubt and flush it down the toilet! You have accomplished an incredible feat to date and have the ability, grit, and determination to make it through any part of the Trail. Just be smart about it, especially when there are wet rocks, and you will do fine. Don't beat yourself up either if you get a little behind schedule. All you can do is give it your best effort! Keep it up!

JR

Tom S

Congrats again for finishing two-thirds of the trail! By today you'll have walked 70 percent-plus of the total miles. Keep your confidence up. You've been able to handle all that the Trail has thrown you way so far. Walking with you page by page and day by day. I have the easy part!

Tom S.

Massachusetts lake view from the Trail.

Day 57: Audio Books

Miles Hiked: 27
Total Miles: 1550.5
Banked Miles: 163.9

07/18/2017

Today I had none of three things that really bother me. The Trail had big climbs, but they were pretty much all on dirt and not rocks (or wet rocks). I wore a lot of Deep Woods Off and so the bugs were not too bad, and when they were, I wore my head net. It was hot, but not too hot. I stopped at twenty-seven miles today because the next road crossing was farther than I wanted to go. I did accidentally start hiking southbound for around a quarter of a mile today. It made me so mad when I realized what I had done. It was also in a difficult area. My big thing today is that I started to listen to audio books while I walk by myself. It is big because I do not believe in headphones (earbuds) while running or hiking. I believe they are dangerous, particularly for females, because you cannot hear what is going on around you. I tried to justify it in my mind by only wearing it in one ear, so I can still hear everything around me, and thinking that it will help keep the gnats buzzing out of that ear. It really bothered me a lot that I was doing it, but it also really helped pass the time today while hiking alone. I made it over 1,500 miles without any stimulus like this—time to move on I guess.

3 Comments

Sue D

Nothing like a good audio book! Enjoy! Your progress has been phenomenal. Stay strong and positive. Or not. You're doing great!!!

Steve H

I'm of the same mind for running and walking with headphones on. I think it is important to be able to hear around you, especially for safety with cars if you are crossing some roads and approaching bikes if you are on a mixed trail (neither of which applies to you right now!). This spring, I did break down and wear one earbud on some long runs (2–3 hours) when training for my June marathon. It did help pass the time as I generally get a bit bored on those long jaunts. Mixing it up is a good thing—keeps the grind to a minimum. Keep up the great work and entertaining posts!

Rick

Wow! One earphone in—you really live dangerously, my friend! Keep it up!
Rick

Me, Martha, Marty, and Elizabeth.

Day 58: Liking MA now

Miles Hiked: 27.2
Total Miles: 1577.7
Banked Miles: 166.8

07/19/2017

Today was a really good day. I decided to start a little late (7:30) because it rained so hard last night, I wanted to give the rocks a little time to dry. The terrain was peaceful and smooth all day. My Aunt Martha came to see me again and with her this time was her daughter Elizabeth and son Marty. They hiked in with Mick to meet me and then we hiked out together. We then went and found a very good Italian restaurant in a small Berkshire town where I proceeded to have a strawberry smoothie, a meatball grinder, and fried donut holes. Now full, we then went back to the Trail and they continued to hike with me and Mick for two more legs. That is hard to do. I so much appreciated and enjoyed their company. Once we parted ways at 5 p.m., I still had to do around nine more miles to get over a mountain to reach the town of Cheshire, Massachusetts. Mick walked in to meet me at the top and we got back to the van at around 8:45 p.m. I then proceeded to polish off the homemade pizza Cathy had made for me a few days ago in Connecticut. She also made me an awesome turkey chili that I polished off yesterday. It has been so nice to have some days with good weather, few bugs, few rocks, and great relatives.

My father moved to Natick, MA from GA when he was thirteen and continued to live in the state through Harvard and Harvard Law School. I usually came to Natick at least once a year to visit my grandparents. Although I am much further west on the hike, it still has a familiar feel that I like a lot.

Uncle Kevin and Aunt Val.

Day 59: Into Vermont

Miles Hiked: 21.7
Total Miles: 1599.4
Banked Miles: 164.2

07/20/2017

The terrain got tougher today. There were a lot of very steep ups and downs. Some of the sections had rocks I had to climb up and some sections were relatively smooth, but a lot less smooth than the last few days. In the end I was pretty wiped out early today (around 5:30 p.m.) with a choice of doing an additional eleven miles before dark or wait until the morning. I chose tomorrow morning. The fun part of the day was seeing my wife's Uncle Kevin and Aunt Val. Kevin is a really experienced hiker, having done all the high peaks in the Adirondacks in both summer and winter. They both hiked in towards me, with Mick going up towards Mt. Greylock, and then we all hiked back down. We had lunch together near Williamstown, Massachusetts before heading back to the Trail, where Kevin again hiked with me for a while before returning to their car. I talked to Kevin about some of my apprehension about New Hampshire and Maine, and he tried to reassure me that I could do it, which was helpful. A few miles into this leg of the hike, I passed the sign saying I was in Vermont. I am starting to see southbound hikers. They start in Maine in June because Mt. Katahdin isn't open until then because of snow. I have noticed a lot of female southbounders. I think I see around one or two in ten that are females hiking northbound.

My younger daughter Caroline went to the UK today for a summer program. Although I am on the AT and have not gotten to see her much lately, it was still hard for me today knowing that she will be so far away without me or my wife. She will not be back until after I (hopefully) finish the hike.

Pretty stream near Williamstown, Massachusetts.

Small muddy stretch.

Day 60: A Tough Mudder

Miles Hiked: 33.7
Total Miles: 1633
Banked Miles: 173.6

07/21/2017

It was a long day. My first leg of the hike was eleven miles, and the second was 22.7 miles, as those were the distances between road crossings. I knew it was going to be hard (but never sure how hard), so I got started at 5:30 a.m. (finished at 7 p.m.). My impression so far of Vermont is that it is really muddy. I prefer muddy to rocky, but it is hard to describe just how muddy it is (though I will try). It is a deep, black mud. It is hard to tell the water/mud mix until you step in it. The mud on the Trail can last for several yards to several hundred yards before some relief only to be back in it in another twenty yards. Today's hike really reminded me of the "tough mudder" obstacle course race craze. These races are often 5K, but they have the participant running through mud and water, up and over things and under things. My hike was kind like that for thirty-three miles. My bug spray seems to be keeping the mosquitos away from me. The weather has been very moderate.

I met a guy today whose trail name is Voyager. He is completing his second triple crown (AT, PCT, and CDT) at the age of 63. I also walked past a thru-hiker today who had to be in his mid to late 70s. I should have asked him his age.

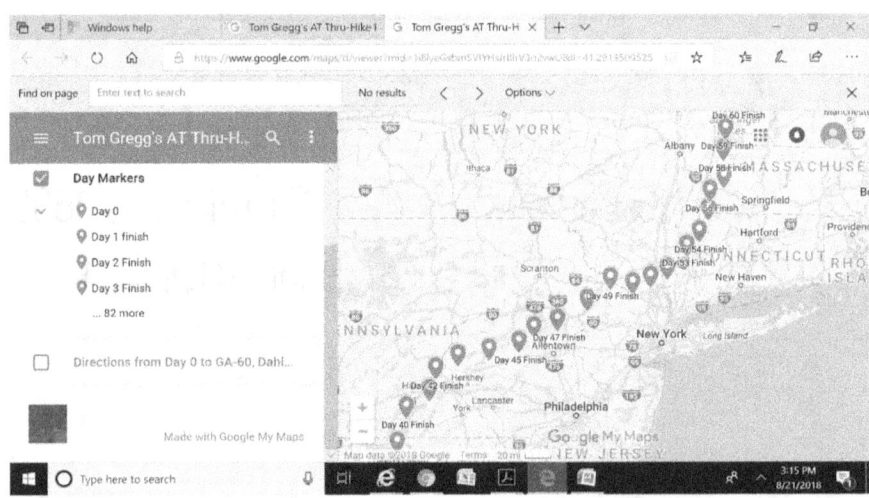

This is how I went through PA, NJ, NY, CT and MA.

OK, Vermont is not all mud.

Day 61: Vermud

Miles Hiked: 23
Total Miles: 1656.1
Banked Miles: 172.3

07/22/2017

I started around 6:20 this morning, but I only hiked twenty-three miles today because the next road crossing was 12.5 miles and I did not want to hike over thirty-five miles today as the terrain was a little too difficult. My first leg today was 17.5 miles, so it took me the entire morning. Mick hiked in a few miles and brought me an egg, cheese, and bacon sandwich and let me know there were donuts to be had when I made it back to the van. This is good incentive. The Trail was still real muddy again, so it slowed me down a little, but as I was only going twenty-three miles, it did not bother me much. I awoke to cool temperatures in the 50s. It took me a few minutes to get used to it when I started (and it warmed-up), but cool temperatures are good for me for hiking. The high where I am now will only be 56 on Monday.

Today I was thinking about my Chinese friend and business partner Henry's mother. I met her for the first time when she invited me over for dinner thirty years ago in the city of Chengdu. I was teaching at a university there at the time and Henry was a graduate student and new friend. She stood less than five feet tall, but had a big and happy personality. She was so nice to me then. When Henry and I started a business to help Americans do business in China a few years later, she would always accompany us when I was in town. She did not have to do this. She was a very important woman in China at the time, and to make time for Henry and me was a big deal. Once, the three of us took a five-hour car ride together, with Henry driving, me in the passenger seat, and his mother in the back. She talked to me in Chinese the entire way. I understood maybe 50 percent, but she ended each sentence with yes or no, agree or disagree, or is or is not. I would make a choice and then look at Henry to get his nod if I was right or quickly change my answer when he shook his head no. She was always so nice and kind to me, I like to consider her my Chinese mother. I have not seen her in many years, but Henry assures me she is doing well.

2 Comments

Uncle Ken

Great progress, Cool Breeze. You just passed the three-quarters mark.

You are really seeing elevation change. Over your last two legs in VT you've made over 12K feet ascent and 12K feet descent, according to http://www.atdist.com.

P.S. And I love the name of your stop: "Mad Tom Notch".

buddy t

Tom,

Still so impressed with your perseverance and determination. Hang tough and finish strong. You're in great position for an achievement few others have pulled off!

Vermont pond.

Day 62: Harry Potter

07/23/2017

Miles Hiked: 28.8

Total Miles: 1684.9

Banked Miles: 176.8

I started this morning at 6am at Mad Tom Notch—how appropriate. I did around twenty miles in my first two legs this morning. As it was Saturday, I saw a lot of weekend day hikers. It was a lot less muddy today in the area I hiked and everyone seemed to be happy to be out there, with temperatures in the 60s. Both my daughters Sara and Caroline and my nieces Elisabeth and Courtney love Harry Potter, and as I have never read it, suggested that I listen to it while I hike. So, today I got a good way through the first book with one earphone in and one free to listen to nature and other hikers. The day seemed to go a lot faster listening to the wizardly adventures. It is pretty impressive how one reader can do so many voices in an audio book.

2 Comments

Sue D

Looks like it was a beautiful day! Harry Potter works wonders for the soul. Enjoy! You're doing great!

Steve H

Jim Dale is masterful with his delivery of Harry Potter. Enjoy the physical scenery of the hike and the mental scenery of Hogwarts!

(That mud does not sound fun.)

Day 63: Oh Happy Day

Miles Hiked: 30.5
Total Miles: 1715.4
Banked Miles: 183

Late last night my wife arrived to visit me here in Vermont. I am so happy to have her here. I had gotten rooms for us and Mick in a nice Inn in a town called Mendon. Tonight we are staying in an inn in the town of Woodstock, and tomorrow we will likely be in Hanover, New Hampshire, home of Dartmouth University. I got going really early this morning to get through Killington Mountain so I could meet my wife for lunch (we found a nice Irish pub). In seventh grade I went to Killington with the Cabin John Jr. High Ski Club. It was the year after I learned to ski in Aspen with my Aunt Nancy. I was going to show everyone what a great skier I was. When I got there, it was 20 degrees below zero on top and it was a total sheet of ice. I would take the chair lift up the bunny slope with the face mask I had to purchase and make one trip down the ice and then into the restaurant for a hot chocolate. It was a little different this time, and I was at the top of the mountain before I knew it. I ended-up going a little farther than I wanted trying to find a good road crossing where Mick could get us back to Woodstock at the end of the day. There were some pretty steep climbs today, but not much in terms of rocks, bugs, or heat (or even mud), so I did not mind at all. My wife found a good restaurant and got some food to go and we had a picnic by a river in Woodstock around 8:30 p.m. when I got done with hiking. Then, our day concluded with ice cream at the local shop.

At an Irish pub for lunch.

Breakfast—not bad for the Trail?

Day 64: Near 0 day

07/25/2017

Miles Hiked: 9
Total Miles: 1724.4
Banked Miles: 167.7

I decided last night that I would stay at the Jackson House Inn for breakfast, which did not start until 8:15 a.m. The owner of the Inn prepared a two-course meal done mostly sous-vide. He announced that he got his buttermilk at the same farm where Chef Thomas Keller of French Laundry and Per Se fame exclusively gets his butter. Chef Keller was a partner chef for a company I ran as a subsidiary for Cuisine Solutions called Fiveleaf. He is a great person. The food and ambiance today was quite a dichotomy from how I have been living on the AT. It was a hard drive in the van down from where I stopped last night, so my wife agreed to take me back in her rental car after breakfast. We decided to take another way up the mountain in the hope that it was a better road. It was, until around 1.6 miles from the Trail, where we could go no further. The road had become a rocky path. So, I had to hike back up the mountain. Did I mention it was raining—hard? It took me close to an hour to walk to the Trail through deep streams of rainwater coming off the mountain, using my Guthook app for directional guidance the whole way. It was a little scary. Once on the Trail, things were back to normal. I'd bought some new trail shoes the other day at a Dick's in one of the towns. They were advertised as lightweight with "mega traction". I tried them for 3 miles yesterday on the dry trail and there was not much cushioning, and the verdict was out on the traction. Today on the wet rocks, they did great—super great. I will sacrifice some comfort for safety. This was a good test for the hard rocky climbs I will be getting to soon in New Hampshire and Maine. When I got finished with the nine AT miles, I decided that that was enough, and I would spend the remainder of the day with my wife. We all had a quick lunch in the van that she had gotten in Woodstock, VT, and we took off for a fun afternoon. I had booked another night at the same inn. We spoke to my daughter Caroline in England on WhatsApp and Facetime with our daughter Sara back in VA. It was such a nice afternoon and evening. It will be very sad when she leaves tomorrow. This was only my second near-zero mile day. The first was a long time ago, in Gatlinburg, TN.

A rainy day on the Trail.

Day 65: Welcome to NH

07/26/2017

Miles Hiked: 30.8
Total Miles: 1755.2
Banked Miles: 174.2

It was very difficult saying goodbye to my wife this morning. Although Vermont turned-out to be a really nice state to hike despite the mud, my wife's visit was the highlight. I started hiking around 6:30 a.m. and kept going until around 7:30 p.m. It was raining a little this morning and I kept coming out of the mountain forests into meadows which are normally good, but when it is wet, they soak you through from shoe to chest, like you are walking through a stream. I got into Hanover, New Hampshire (Dartmouth University) under cloudy skies at around 3 p.m. This is the third time I have been to Hanover. The first time was in 2004, when we came to visit Don't Mind and Don't Matter (Lisa and Kit) on their AT thru-hike. The second time was to show my girls Dartmouth around four or five years ago. My car broke down on a Sunday at a gas station in Hanover and there was nowhere to get it fixed. I vowed never to come back. I had to walk out of town to see if another service station was open or not, and it was the same route as the AT that I hiked today. I no longer harbor a grudge with the town. I talked on the phone with Don't Mind and Don't Matter this evening. I have so many questions of the upcoming 226 miles of really difficult terrain (the White Mountains and beyond); I will get to that section in another one-and-a-half days. They were very encouraging and patient as I asked question after question. You will soon start to see why I have saved so many banked miles.

One Comment

Sue D
> Love Hanover and Dartmouth! I coached there for a couple years in the early 90s—lived across the river in Norwich, VT. Great photo! You're doing great! So fun to see your progress. One step at a time!

Early morning from up high

Day 66: I wore my backpack

07/27/2017

Miles Hiked: 25.2

Total Miles: 1780.4

Banked Miles: 175.1

So, as I reach the White Mountains tomorrow, there will be fewer and fewer road crossings and there may be a time that I will have to wear a regular backpack and carry more gear and supplies. I decided to practice today. This is the first time I have worn my backpack on the entire hike. It was very hard for me. I am not sure if it was the terrain or the pack: I did not put anything in the pack except what I always carry, but the pack itself is around double the weight of what I normally carry. I was doing a fourteen-mile stretch, with two steep mountains to climb, and I had already completed one and was about to start the second in a tired and demoralized state when I ran into a father with his thirteen- and fourteen-year old boys who were thru-hiking the AT. We struck-up a conversation and ended up walking up and down the second mountain together. I walked much more slowly than usual (it took a lot longer), but I forgot all about the weight of my pack and the difficulty of the climb and descent. The father had retired from the Marines and NATO, but he and his wife and four kids still lived in Belgium. The two boys hiking, Stretch and Re-mix, both spoke German, French, and Dutch—as well as English. We swapped stories for a long time and when we got back to the van, we got out the folding chairs and we all ate and drank Trail magic from the van. A pickup truck pulled up to us as we sat and invited all of us to stay at the house of a former governor of NH (I think) up the street who produces his own maple syrup. My new friends had read all about this person and place and graciously accepted his invitation. Mick and I declined, and we said our goodbyes. They are raising money to fight Alzheimer's as part of their hike (hikefor.com).

Stretch, Remax, and I with my backpack.

2 Comments

Tom
    80 percent completed! Steady as she goes! It's not a race, but a journey.

Alex
    I would've gone for some maple syrup.

The Omelet Man.

Day 67: Grandma Smithwood to the rescue

Miles Hiked: 12
Total Miles: 1792.4
Banked Miles: 162.8

07/28/2017

Rain and thunderstorms were predicted today, so I decided it was not the day to start the difficult White Mountains and I would dip into my Banked Miles account. I will start them tomorrow morning with the additional support of my in-laws, Grandma Smithwood and Ron (need to give him a trail name also), and Mick will hike with me. I was in a panic this morning when I realized I had made a reservation in a White Mountains hut, and I would no longer be able to get there in time. I will need to sleep in the mountain huts, which require reservations, because of the lack of road crossings, but we drove this morning around twenty minutes until we could get some cell reception and the Appalachian Mountain Club agreed to shift my dates. I was lucky, as they usually do not have the availability this time of year to make a change like this, and I do not know what I would have done if I could not have gotten in a hut for certain nights ahead. I will talk more about them in future entries. As I did not have to go far today, I got started late and within a half-mile on the Trail ran into The Omelet Man. This man provides Trail magic (breakfast) for free to all hikers that walk by, seven days a week. This is quite a big and cool thing. He was very nice and explained how rewarding it was to him meeting so many interesting people. I only had a little juice and a muffin and was on my way. Grandma Smithwood and Ron met us at Glencliff, NH at 2 p.m. in the light rain.

It was great seeing them. After a few stories, I walked another mile or so up the mountain to the last parking lot so tomorrow won't be quite so long a day, and they went and got me a vanilla milkshake. We all then drove into Lincoln, NH, where they are staying, and had a really nice dinner. I will tell you more about how they will support us in my next entry.

Grandma Smithwood and Ron with me and Mick.

Mick coming down some rocks.

Day 68: Man of Wheel

Miles Hiked: 23.5
Total Miles: 1815.9
Banked Miles: 162

07/29/2017

Today was by far the hardest day on the Trail. There were several occasions during the day that I was thinking about packing it in and going home. The first was the 4,000 foot climb that Mick and I started at 5:45 a.m. that was so steep. I knew it was going to be steeper coming down, and the rocks were wet and it looked like it was going to storm. After weathering that eight-mile part of the hike, we then began a sixteen-mile leg that was essentially rock climbing for over 8 hours (which I am not good at). In all, I got 23.5 miles in twelve-plus hours of hiking. This all may be too much for me. I am going to be carrying my own stuff the next two days (which will make it even harder) and staying in huts along the way. Tomorrow will be twenty miles through the Franconia Ridge area and then fifteen miles to part way up Mt. Washington. I do not think I will be able to write this journal for a while.

The saving grace today was Grandma Smithwood and The Man of Wheel (Ron's new trail name, as he can drive anything with four wheels, and is like Superman to us). They waited for us at the two road crossings so Mick could go with me, which I needed so much. Mick is a little beaten-up now, as that was his longest hike and it was so hard. He will get a little break now as I will stay in huts for the next two days.

3 Comments

Sue D

Tremendous feat! You're a rockstar! (Pun intended) One step at a time!

Alexandra

You'll make it through. Take a breather and enjoy it. Less than four hundred miles to go. Then you can plan your Rocky Mountain hike!

Uncle Ken

What a monster day! Over those 23.5 miles you had 9,360 feet of ascent and 8,960 feet of descent, totaling 18,000 feet of elevation changes. A hiking rule of thumb is to plan one hour for every three miles in distance, plus one hour for every two thousand feet of elevation change. So your trip would be estimated to require seventeen hours. You are doing great, keep it slow and steady.

And I really like that you brought in the big guns—Grandma Smithwood and the Man of Wheel!

Franconia Ridge.

Day 69: Spectacular Views

Miles Hiked: 20.1
Total Miles: 1838.6
Banked Miles: 157.8

07/30/2017

The weather was perfect today making it a little easier, but it was still very, very hard compared to any other place on the Trail. I had spectacular views for several exposed miles of the hike along Franconia Ridge. Today I carried my own backpack, which was a lot more weight than I am used to, but far less than most backpackers carry. I brought a chicken wrap, but I also stopped at a hut along the way and got tomato soup, two Snickers, and two cups of lemonade. Tonight I stayed in a full-service hut called Zealand. I have a bunk with a pillow and 3 wool blankets, and they served a camp-like dinner, and I will get breakfast. The best thing recently for my hiking has been my new Merrell trail shoes that I got at Dick's, with the mega traction. They have made a huge difference.

The hard climbing I discussed.

Day 70: A shorter day

Miles Hiked: 14.2
Total Miles: 1850.8
Banked Miles: 147.7

07/31/2017

I had a nice Sunday breakfast of bacon and eggs at 7 a.m. at Zealand Hut and got on my way at 7:30. I walked eight miles down to Mick, and it was super smooth. I couldn't believe it. I was back to three miles per hour. After a quick early lunch of a burger, tots, and a milkshake that Mick had picked up for me, and a few minutes to post my journal, I got back on the Trail for just six more miles up to Mizpah Hut. It was the opposite of this morning. The first four or five miles felt like pure rock climbing, made harder by the fact that I was carrying a backpack. I had plenty of time to make it, as I started at noon, but that did not seem to make it any easier. Mick decided that he wanted to climb Mt. Washington with me tomorrow, so he drove the van the thirty-six road miles to the next road crossing and then got a ride back to a place with a trail that was only a 2.5 mile hike to Mizpah Hut. He arrived before I did. We had a nice dinner here. I got a bottom-level bunk today which is much better than my third level bunk last night. We are going to get an early start tomorrow. . . .

One Comment

Uncle Ken

    Cool Breeze, the trees in that picture look kind of funny, the way they grow horizontal to the rocky pathway. Oh wait, unless the trees are growing vertical, which means the rocks....

Atop Mt. Washington.

Day 71: Mt. Washington

Miles Hiked: 19.6
Total Miles: 1870.4
Banked Miles: 143

08/01/2017

We decided to leave at 6:15 a.m. this Monday. The staff at Mizpah Hut agreed to make us some eggs at 6 a.m. before we left (breakfast is not until 7 a.m.). We knew the first eight-tenths of a mile was steep, with some rock climbing, but it was OK hiking for the first six miles after that, around some Presidential mountains, and then straight up to the top of Mt. Washington (6,288 feet). We were there before 9 a.m. It was sunny and clear until we got to the very top, where it became foggy. I was all right with that. At the snack bar, I ate two cinnamon donuts, two bags of Fritos and an orange soda. In all, I had thirteen miles of exposure today (above tree line). I wanted to get through that before the potential thunderstorm. On our second six-mile leg, Mick's knee started to hurt again. As it was weak and we were walking on what I would describe as the surface of the moon (rocks), he started twisting his ankle a lot. He had to slow way down. When we got to Madison Hut, we each had a bowl of lentil soup, and we made the decision that he could not do the next difficult eight-and-a-half miles. There was a three-mile Valley Trail that he could take down, and then try to get a ride to Pinkham Notch, where he had parked the car and I would meet him. It still took him over three hours to get down. I climbed Mt. Pierce, and then walked slowly along the ridgeline on difficult rocks and few areas where my fear of heights started to come to the surface, but not too bad. Once I was back in the trees, the trail was steep, but I did not find it too difficult, as there were fewer rocks than above the tree line. Around 4:30, as I was getting close to Pinkham Notch, I started hearing thunder and seeing some lightning. I was very happy I was no longer at the top in the exposed area. When I got to the parking lot at 5 p.m., the van was right by the AMC Visitor's Center (not where Mick told me), so I knew he had gotten back and moved it. As I approached the van, the rain started to fall—what perfect timing.

As we were leaving the summit of Mt. Washington, we saw the first of three cog trains coming up the mountain. I still remember riding up Mt. Washington on the cog train when I was five years old. My grandparents and parents had rented a cabin on a mountain with a lake somewhere in New Hampshire for a month. The three things I remember most about that trip was that I learned to play chess (and wanted to play all the time;

my grandfather (dad's father), who along with my grandmother were the nicest and most fun people in the world, tried to teach me how to fish; and my dad took me to climb Little Wildcat Mountain. I think we made it to the top—at least that is what he told me. Tomorrow I will climb two Wildcat mountains. It is supposed to be the toughest six miles on the Trail (Mahoosic Notch coming up in Maine is also known as the toughest mile). So, I was thinking of taking a rest day tomorrow (zero day), but instead I am going to do the hard six miles and then stay overnight at the Carter Notch Hut and make it a "nero day" (near zero miles). I will meet Mick fifteen miles down the Trail the following day.

The Mt. Washington cog train.

One Comment

Catherine L

Wow! Hoping you can get some much deserved rest this afternoon and that Mick's knee is doing okay. Glad the huts are working out for you and you get to experience another aspect of the Trail. Keep on truckin', Tom, you are amazing!

Socks and I, at Carter Notch Hut.

Day 72: The Wildcats

08/02/2017

Miles Hiked: 5.9

Total Miles: 1876.3

Banked Miles: 124.6

As I only had to do six miles today, I slept in this Tuesday morning and Mick and I had breakfast at the Appalachian Mountain Club (AMC) Visitor Center. I started hiking the Wildcats at around 10 a.m. and quickly met another thru-hiker, "Socks," as we both followed several other hikers the wrong way up a steep rocky hill. Socks is a 65-year-old hiker from Tacoma, WA, who is finishing the entire AT for the second time. He has hiked and biked all over the US. It took us almost four hours to complete the six miles. There was a lot of rock climbing involved. I had written in my notes from my AT school that this was the hardest six miles on the Trail, and Don't Mind (Lisa) confirmed this to me over the phone last week when I called Don't Matter (Kit) for advice. It went a lot easier hiking with someone. I had made a reservation at Carter Notch Hut (the last hut in the system) at the end of the six miles, and decided to really rest this afternoon. The kitchen at the hut didn't have lunch, but I was able to get a bowl of thick potato dill soup, a couple big slices of cake, and two cups of hot chocolate. A group of teens from Overland (a summer travel program that my daughters and nieces and nephew have done) were also staying at the hut. I passed them yesterday climbing Mt. Washington. Tomorrow is their last day but it is very impressive what they have done. Socks was able to do a "work for stay" arrangement at the hut, so he will walk with me tomorrow to the next road crossing.

Pond in front of Carter Notch Hut.

View from top of Carter Dome.

Day 73: Finished the White Mountains

08/03/2017

Miles Hiked: 16.1

Total Miles: 1892.4

Banked Miles: 116.4

I started at 6:15 a.m. this Wednesday morning to try to get done before the mid-day predicted storms. I started walking up the very steep Carter Dome with Socks, but he could not keep up with me today, and I soon was on my own. However, at the top of the mountain, I met another fast hiker named French Press, and he and I walked together for a while until he wanted to stop for water, and I decided to continue again on my own as I really wanted to beat the rain and avoid the slippery rocks. I completed the sixteen miles at around 1 p.m., just beating the rain again. We put out the awning on the van and waited for the other thru-hikers to make it down so they had some protection from the rain and some Trail magic (food and drink). We got to socialize with a bunch of people for a while, which was very fun, and 2.5 hours later Socks made it down and we drove him with us to town for dinner. Mick's knee is still bothering him, but he walked in a mile or so to test it. This next section as I enter Maine will be a real test for me. There are no road crossings for thirty-one miles, and it is really hard terrain, with storms predicted. Mahoosic Notch is billed by many as the toughest (or most fun) one mile on the Trail, as it requires having to climb over, under, and around big boulders. I am going to break the hike into two days and do Mahoosic on the second, with fresh legs I think, so either I tent camp for the first time tomorrow with Mick, or I do an extra 4 miles off a mountain to get to the van and back the next day. Stay tuned.

4 Comments

Catherine L
> SO glad you've had a couple of good strong days and hiking companions to help pass the time. Kudos to you, too, for giving yourself extra time to recuperate. Hoping Mahoosic Notch is more fun than scary! You've got this, Tom!

Sue D
> Gorgeous view from Carter Dome! Hard to believe it's August and you're almost to Maine. You're doing great, Tommy!

Alexandra D
> Do the extra 4 miles and camp in the van. You know that's more comfortable. We've got 2 more routes for you to map out . . . the Eclipse route and the Rocky Mountain

Trail. Rest up!

Jennifer G

Tom,

I just talked to Mom and read her the last couple of your days over the phone! She kept saying "good" when you mentioned resting. Ha ha. Meanwhile, I was jealous of all the junk food you are having.

We love you and are so proud of all you have accomplished. You are in the home stretch of your journey, so enjoy every minute (even if it's painful) and think about how good it will feel to finish! Plus, you get to see me at the end! BONUS! I can't wait to see you in couple weeks!! Also, I can fill you in on all you missed on this season of *The Bachelorette*. Ha ha! KEEP PUSHING! #1!

Love you so much,

Jenn Jenn

Day 74: Maine

Miles Hiked: 16.1
Total Miles: 1908.5
Banked Miles: 108.2

08/04/2017

I started early today at around 6 a.m. as thunderstorms and rain was predicted for the afternoon starting at 1 p.m. I wanted to get through as much as I could before the rain because I knew I would be on very difficult rocks. I crossed into Maine around 1 p.m. and I could feel raindrops. At that point, I only had half a mile to go before my turn-off to get back to the van, as we had planned. The rain started to come down hard, so I put on my rain jacket and then got to do a few very difficult rock descents on the wet rocks. I was happy the hiking day was almost over. It would have been really difficult to continue. As I started off on the side trail to the van, I saw Mick walking towards me. He walked the two miles up to me on his bum knee and let me know the trail to the van was pretty easy. It took me around eight hours to do the sixteen miles, plus the two miles to the van. I will likely get up early again tomorrow and try to get through the challenging Mahoosuc Notch early, before the thunderstorms and rains come again as predicted. It is around six miles away. The goal is to get there after the rocks have dried from today's rain and before tomorrow's rain. It will be a very difficult day if the rocks are wet tomorrow. I met and hiked for a while today with a guy named One Gallon from Iowa. He has three hiking triple crowns and is finishing his fourth AT thru-hike at the age of fifty-seven. I am told by other hikers he is a legend. I have seen a lot of the same people lately as I have been going so much slower (fewer miles) lately. I usually see someone once (maybe twice) and I am gone.

Cool Breeze and One Gallon.

Day 75: Mahoosuc Notch

Miles Hiked: 14.1
Total Miles: 1922.6
Banked Miles: 98

08/05/2017

Friday was quite a day. To say it was hard does not do it justice. Actually, the Mahoosuc Notch ended up being one of the easier parts of the hike. I started today at 5:45 a.m. There were thunderstorms in the forecast from noon through the night, so I wanted to get as far as I could before they hit. I had to do my two miles up the mountain from the van to the Trail (so I really did 16.1 miles). I then proceeded nervously towards the Mahoosuc Notch. It was around six miles away. As it rained yesterday afternoon and evening, all the rocks were wet and slippery. I have gained a lot of experience this last week or so, and I have learned to really use the trees and roots to help pull me up climbs. There were a lot of climbs I was pulling myself up the rock ledges anyway I could. As I got closer to the Notch (like a valley), I caught up with One Gallon again (he got his name for eating an entire gallon of ice cream at one sitting). Who better to hike the hardest one mile on the trail than with the hiking legend who has already done it three times. It was so lucky for me. Mahoosuc Notch was a rock obstacle course. It was far from the hardest mile for me, but it may have been the longest mile by time as you had to think through every obstacle. Luckily, One Gallon would go first, and I would follow his lead. Often, he would see a better way once he had done it that I would then take. As I did not have a big pack to get through some of the tunnels, I had a much easier time of it. The hike out of the Notch (up, up, up) was much harder on the slippery slate. I tried to go as fast as I could because I knew it would be worse if it started to rain. One Gallon eventually took a break and I kept going. I owe him a dinner at Medium Rare or something. . . . When I got to within thirty minutes of Grafton Notch, where the van was parked, I met up with Mick and a band of around eight other northbound thru-hikers. We all hiked down the mountain together. It was the first easier terrain of the day. Everyone was exhausted and it was just 3 p.m. (nine hours for me). I would have to do another ten miles to the next road crossing, but I did not think I wanted to do it with the potential thunderstorms and my sore body, so I am using some more of my banked miles.

One Comment

Caryn
    Sounds like smart hiking all around. Stay strong, Tom!

Day 76: Beat out the rain

Miles Hiked: 19.6
Total Miles: 1942.2
Banked Miles: 93.3

08/06/2017

The forecast for Saturday, August 5 was heavy rains all day. I decided that I would get up early and do ten miles, no matter how hard or slippery. I left at 5:45 and it was not yet raining. It was very foggy and the rocks were still wet from the rain from last evening. The first climb was extremely hard, but I got through it. The wind was blowing really hard on top of the mountain, but that dried off all the exposed rock, making it a little easier to climb. After the ten miles, I got back in the van to decide whether or not I could do another ten miles. It started to rain and I was ready to quit for the day (it was only 11 a.m.), and then One Gallon walked up to the van and he said he was continuing. After around another 30 minutes of indecision, I decided to go for it. It only rained for around fifteen minutes after I began hiking, and then it stopped for the rest of the hike. I met One Gallon again after six miles, and we hiked together the difficult final four miles. I have been listening to Harry Potter when I am hiking alone. Today, Book Four, featured Professor Moody, and I was climbing Moody Mountain. After we got back to the van and headed to the town of Andover, the rain started to come down hard. It is like a flash flood outside as I write this. I really dodged a bullet today, weather-wise. I cannot wait to get out of these mountains.

2 Comments

Catherine L

> Tom, so happy to hear from you again! Sounds like you did an awesome job conquering Mahoosic Notch and all of the other challenges these past few days. Isn't it amazing how One Gallon showed up at just the right time to help you out? Hoping there is less rain in the coming days and that Mick's knee is feeling better. Sara arrived today here in Guilford. We are all thinking of you! Xoxo, Cathy

Tom S

> Glad you are back on the grid! Made your last State and after today around 90 percent done! I know you lived a couple years in Paris, but in your remaining many hours of hiking it may be a good time to start practicing your French. In particular, two words. I understand that it tastes just as good out of fine crystal glasses or a plastic cup. Safe travels.

Berries on the Trail.

Day 77: Pushing Through

Miles Hiked: 26.4
Total Miles: 1968.6
Banked Miles: 95.4

08/07/2017

I was a little nervous as I had to do more than twenty-six miles today, and I haven't done that for a while because of the difficult terrain. The weather forecast was for a sunny day so I set off at 6 a.m. with no jacket, and I forgot my cap. It turned out to be a windy day and I was literally in the clouds for a good while, which was a little moist. As the first road crossing was thirteen miles away (six hours in this terrain), I probably should have brought a rain jacket to be safe. I caught up with One Gallon again after around four miles, and we hiked together the rest of the leg, and four miles into my second thirteen-mile leg. The first leg was pretty difficult, with some steep rocky climbs and some very steep rocky descents. I go much slower hiking with One Gallon, which is also much safer, so I hardly noticed most of it while we chatted. The second leg was the easiest terrain I have had since I entered New Hampshire, which seems like a long time ago. I mostly spent the thirteen miles trying not to walk through mud bogs and puddles which punctuated this walk. There were many beautiful lakes and ponds the whole way. I parted company with One Gallon after four miles into the second leg, as that is where he was stopping for the day. I will probably not see him again as I am now 9 miles ahead. It was very cool and lucky to have hiked for around three days with one of the most "hiker" famous guys on the Trail in the most difficult sections. If the weather holds out for me, I may be able to finish the most difficult 226 miles of the Trail in another two days. Keep your fingers crossed for me.

5 Comments

Uncle Ken

Way to go, Cool Breeze! Less than three miles for you to pass the 90 percent mark!

Kevin D

Tom—you are doing phenomenal. Just as I thought, the Trail is not giving you problem feelings of heights.

BTW – those berries in your photo today are of a trout lily.http://1.bp.blogspot.com/-guubyxEEaU/UgtvSv8nIoI/AAAAAAAABO4/DoARZ5Xf7bY/s1600/Erythronium+americanum+-+Trout+Lily+09.JPG

I tried to put in a link to a photo here, but I don't think it worked. You could look it up online. They are very pretty.

Dan

Amazing accomplishment already, Tom. You're on the homestretch . . . best wishes for the Trail ahead. Enjoy!

Marcie M

You are doing so well!!!! Keep it up and I can't wait to hear some great stories when we celebrate your return.

Tom S

Just looked at the seven-to-ten day forecast for Mt. Katahdin and it indicated that a "Cool Breeze" was heading its way! Go Dog Go!

On top of Saddleback Mountain in southern Maine.

Day 78: Weather held out

08/08/2017

Miles Hiked: 24
Total Miles: 1992.6
Banked Miles: 95.1

Rain was again predicted in the afternoon, so I got going at 6 a.m., as it was a BWRD (Bad Weather Rest Day) in my Appalachian Trail Institute notes. This is because there were several miles of exposure on Saddleback Mountain, which I climbed first today. Like most of the exposed peaks I have encountered lately, there is a cold wind blowing (not a Cool Breeze) and I am often in the clouds, which obstructs the views. Today, I had big winds, but also some clear and spectacular views along a lot of it. Luckily I had my ski cap and raincoat/wind breaker with me today, and I felt pretty confident up there. The descents were pretty steep and difficult again, making for slow going at times, but I made it through. Mick found a logging road where he could walk in half a mile to me at the fifteen mile point to bring me some more food, drink, and socks. The van is also parked around half a mile from the Trail tonight, so I had to do a little extra walking, but it is well worth it to be back in the van (and I have good cell connectivity tonight). Around thirty minutes after getting back to the van around 6 p.m., it finally started to rain. It is predicted to rain all tomorrow, but I am hoping that is wrong. I would really like to finish all (what's billed as) the really hard terrain tomorrow.

2,000 miles marker.

Day 79: 2,000 Miles

Miles Hiked: 24.9
Total Miles: 2017.5
Banked Miles: 95.7

Today (Tuesday) was a big day. I not only crossed the 2,000 miles mark, but also got through the 226 miles of most difficult terrain at the end of the day. I feel really good about that. However, each mile today was very hard. I left the van at 6:30 a.m. It had been raining at 6 a.m. and the weather forecast was for rain all today, and it was wet from the rain last night. It stopped raining as I left the van. It did not rain again all day, and I had sunshine and cool temperatures, probably with a high around 70. Mick met me after around eight miles and then I had seventeen miles after that over the Bigelow Mountains. The views were awesome in the sunshine. Mostly, I get panoramic mountain views, but these were views of both lakes and mountains. I am going to change back to my more comfortable trail shoes tomorrow and give my "great" mega-traction trail shoes a break.

I thought about my mother today (and gave her a call) as I crossed the 2,000 mile mark. My mother really has no clue why I or anyone else would want to do this. My parents still live in the same house I grew up in, in Potomac, MD. My mother was a stay-home mom, although she is well educated and worked in the Harvard Divinity School while my father was in law school. My mother gained an interest in horticulture (azaleas in particular) and antique glass while raising me, my brother John and Sister Jenn. She is now a foremost expert in both areas with a beautiful garden and a huge glass collection. My mother's interests are very different from mine, but I know that she is always there for me and worries about me. She would not have thought any less of me if I had quit this hike after one day. She does not always get the credit she deserves for what she has accomplished, but I think she has accomplished a lot and I want to congratulate her.

From the top of Little Bigelow Mountain.

One Comment

Martha D

Congratulations on achieving this milestone, Tom! I love the post about your Mom. She must be an amazing woman! Marty and I went to the Corning Museum of Glass today. I bet it would be really fun to go there with her! Love, Aunt Martha

Day 80: My Wife's Birthday

Miles Hiked: 25.6
Total Miles: 2043.1
Banked Miles: 97

08/10/2017

I had to walk twenty miles before 1:30 today because the only way I can safely cross the Kennebec River is by canoe, and the canoe man's hours are only 9am–2pm (you must be there half an hour early). So, I left the van at 5:30 this morning. I was feeling so good hiking at a good pace (miles per hour) on a smooth-ish, nice trail. I walked along several really beautiful lakes and a few streams with waterfalls. All was good. I was good and feeling proud of my accomplishments. Then, I looked up when I thought I might have to ford a stream. I did not see a tree stump on its side with long, hard roots sticking out. One caught me in my left leg right below my knee. It punctured my skin, but also sent shock waves throughout my leg. My ankle hurt, my hamstring hurt, my knee hurt, and of course, the point of impact hurt. It reminded me very quickly that I was not finished the AT yet, and one of my important things to remember I list on my journal site—pride goeth before a fall. I started to concentrate again as I limped forward after a few minutes, cursing. I wore my lighter, more comfortable shoes today and felt it helped me move faster. As there were not a lot of rocks, I was fine, but there was an obvious difference in traction. I will not wear these shoes on the upcoming climbs or when it rains. I arrived at the River before 1 p.m. and the canoe man was there waiting for a passenger. The paddle only took around five minutes, but it was quite nice. After getting in the van with Mick around a half-mile later and driving to a place with Internet to post yesterday's journal and eat some lunch, I did another five miles. I decided at that point to stop, although it was still comparatively early, because I had stayed up late last night doing Medium Rare work; I had gotten up at 4:30 this morning, and the next six-mile stretch was up and down a big mountain, which I wanted a break from hiking.

Today is my wife's birthday. I have rarely called her by her name in this journal as she does not like her name used in social media, and I do not think she wants to go by Mrs. Cool Breeze. Missing her birthday is very difficult to me, and it reminds me of the things that I have missed doing this hike. Some of the happiest times I have had on this journey have been when she has visited me. She is in the UK right now with my daughter Caroline looking at prospective universities, so I hope she has had a jolly good birthday with her. Hopefully, we will have time to celebrate her birthday as a family soon after I complete the hike. Having me hike the Trail was never on her wish list, and I truly appreciate her love and encouragement. We have been married for more than twenty-two years, and I look forward to the next twenty-two and beyond. Have a Happy Birthday, and I cannot wait to see you. Love, Tom.

3 Comments

Graceful
> that is a sweet tribute to Mrs. Cool Breeze. What and whom you are missing, you are also appreciating more and more. It's lovely, Tommy!

Alexandra D
> Did you like the video? Happy Birthday to your wife of no name!!

Sue D
> That brought tears to my eyes—not the part about the leg puncture but the part about Mrs. Cool Breeze. Happy birthday!
>
> Go, Tommy, go!

Mick the Moose.

Day 81: Mick the Moose

08/11/2017

Miles Hiked: 31.4

Total Miles: 2074.5

Banked Miles: 104.1

I got started at 5:45 a.m. this morning. I had two mountains to climb and two rivers to ford, but overall it was not a very difficult terrain day. The mountains were not that high and rugged comparatively and I only had to walk ankle deep for around ten feet in both rivers. I did decide to leave my rain jacket behind for the last six miles of the day as it was still sunny, and of course it rained the last hour (but not too hard). Mick spent the day trying to drive to me on very difficult logging roads. He also visited a hiker hostel in Monson to get the skinny on the roads he will need to take in the next section of the hike, called the 100-Miles Wilderness. We are currently parked at the trailhead at the beginning of the 100-Mile Wilderness. I will not see any more towns until after I am done (Mick may see some.). So, we drove into Monson this evening and I loaded the van with all the food and drink that I thought I would need over the next five days. I have a little less than 115 miles to go. Mick and I have been on the lookout for a moose. Mick won and saw one today. I will keep looking. One moose would be plenty for me. I wanted to see a bear and you know how many I ended up seeing. . . .

3 Comments

Jeffrey M
   Incredible journey Tom. You are almost there!!

Alexandra D

Uncle Ken
   We are looking forward to the big finish any day now!

Day 82: It ain't over till it's over

08/12/2017

Miles Hiked: 30.5

Total Miles: 2105

Banked Miles: 110.3

The Trail beat me up today this Friday. I am through the really difficult area, so I was thinking it would not be too bad. The 100-Mile Wilderness is more about the lack of re-supply for backpackers. I was wrong. I checked my school notes when I finally got back to the van at 8:30 p.m. in the dark. It said that it was very rugged, particularly when wet. This is translated into "a lot of rocks." I started out at 6 a.m. and rain was not predicted until 11 a.m., although it started at 9 a.m. I thought the first fifteen miles would be pretty easy and the last fifteen miles would be harder, as it went through a mountain chain with five peaks. However, the first fifteen miles were hard because of the wet rocks. Mick was able to walk into me at mile nine and mile fifteen. It took me so long to get to mile fifteen, I was nervous about getting through the mountains before dark. I had already gashed both my legs in the morning. I tried to go faster in the afternoon, which resulted in three falls. Remember, I only fell once in the first 600 miles, and maybe five or six times before New Hampshire. I have stopped counting now. My pace went from three miles per hour the first seven miles through the mountains to less than two miles per hour for the last eight miles. In the end, I still had to walk the final two miles down off the mountain in the dark with a headlamp. Everything in my body hurts tonight. I have never had a day on the AT where I hurt myself so often and badly.

Steve the Moose.

Day 83: I saw a moose

08/13/2017

Miles Hiked: 21.1

Total Miles: 2126.1

Banked Miles: 107.1

Today (Saturday) was a better day than yesterday. I decided to sleep in a little this morning. I finished last night at a river that I would have to ford first. I wore some water shoes that I changed out of as soon as I got across. It was mainly only around ankle- to shin-deep. I got going around 7:30 a.m. I met a guy after the river crossing whom I walked with for around an hour. He was truly inspiring. He goes by Tin Man because of his heart. He is fifty-five years old and has had a virus in his heart which has made it very weak. He has had dozens of heart attacks. He has been walking over 2,000 miles with a pacemaker and defibrillator. Although I climbed another fifteen-mile mountain range this morning, it was not near as hard as yesterday. I will have no more mountains until the final climb of Mt. Katahdin. As I was going by a little pond about to make my final climb, I saw a moose around 20 feet from me, eating grass. He was very big and would not stop eating so I decided to name him after my business partner, Steve the Moose. He did look up at me, but decided he was not going to do anything different because of me. I am getting close to the end of this journey and I am very excited. I have not had any Internet connection so far in the 100-Mile Wilderness, so I know you will not read this until later.

Mt Katahdin in the distance (I think).

Day 84: We are getting close

08/14/2017

Miles Hiked: 30.4

Total Miles: 2156

Banked Miles: 113.2

I got up early today (Sunday, August 13) as I knew I had to do a lot of miles. I have not been able to get Internet access in the 100-Mile Wilderness, so I know you will see several entry days at the same time. I will try to get Mick to drive me somewhere tomorrow night with Internet access. There is a chance that I could get access at lunch tomorrow, after I hike seventeen miles. The terrain was difficult today in a few places, but it was mostly very nice going by many streams and lakes. Most of my thoughts though while hiking are now are on finishing. I am now also two-thirds of the way of listening to (finishing) the last volume of Harry Potter. It has been difficult not being able to communicate. My daughter Sara is trying to get here for the finish, but it has been a few days since I have been able to talk to her. Mick drove out today to try to make some arrangements for the van at Baxter State Park (Mt. Katahdin) and also to try to reach Sara to coordinate. Hopefully, it will all work out. Unless there is a weather or physical issue, this will probably be the second-to-last entry, as I hope to walk tomorrow and then get to the top of Mt. Katahdin before 10:15 a.m. (the time I started on May 22), so I can count the early morning as part of day 85.

One Comment

Kim W

Congrats Tom! What an amazing accomplishment—and so inspiring. Hope to see you around the 'hood soon.

YES!!!!!!

Day 85: We did it!! Many, many thanks!

08/15/2017

Miles Hiked: 32.5

Total Miles: 2189

Banked Miles: 121.32

I can't believe that I am done. I reached the top of Mt. Katahdin at 9:00 a.m. I am sorry that all these last posts came at the same time, and that I am also writing so much in this last entry. I could not get Internet access at the end of the day anywhere in the 100-Mile Wilderness or Baxter State Park, and the closest town is very far away. Today is Tuesday. I am counting Monday and before 10:15 a.m. on Tuesday as one day, so I completed the Trail in eighty-five days, twenty-two hours and thirty minutes, which I round down to eighty-five days. This means I did an average of twenty-six miles a day (I rounded up a little here), or around a marathon a day for eighty-five days. I am pretty darn happy with this. I am also extremely happy that my regular hiking partner, my daughter Sara, was here to celebrate the finish with me.

I must say that except for the mosquitoes, this is one of the nicest and prettiest areas of the whole Trail, with all the lakes, streams, waterfalls and the beautiful mountain background. The 4,000-foot, very steep climb up Mt. Katahdin today was extremely difficult. I have feared this climb even before starting my hike. However, I knew I had to do it to finish, and I got through it. I did not want to spend too much time at the top (had to get the pictures) as I felt that I was really done when I got back to the van off the steep mountain and was finished hiking. My friend Tom S. not only had shirts made for me (back in Va.), but he also gave me a bottle of Dom to celebrate with when we finished. It was much appreciated and made for a great small celebration. However, Sara had borrowed her Aunt Cathy's car and had a flat tire a mile from my finish, so Mick and some good Samaritans helped us with it and we all celebrated with the champagne when it was fixed.

I decided to write this journal because I like to write, and I wanted to have a record of the hike that I can look back on in the future as memories start to fade. I also wanted to do something where friends, family, and those interested could also follow my journey. Although I like to write, I am far from a professional writer, like my Uncle Mark (among many things, he covered the Apollo missions for the *New York Times*). He is an excellent writer. I worry a little that my unedited copy that I wrote and published at night after a twenty-six mile hike might not meet a very high standard. I know I left out letters, words, spelled things incorrectly, and used bad grammar. Perhaps I will have time to clean it up at some point, but thank you all for getting through it.

    There are so many people I want to thank for their support and encouragement during this hike. First, there is no way I could have done this without the support of Mick. He was with me and helping me every day for eighty-five days. We were a team, and we did it together. I hope he enjoyed getting to see an interesting part of America both by van and hiking on the AT. I want to thank my wife and daughters for all their tolerance and support for me being gone so long and doing this crazy adventure. I want to thank all of my relatives on my side of the family and my wife's family who have been following and supporting me. I want to thank Kit and Lisa for inspiring me from their AT hike in 2004 and coming with me to start my AT hike in Georgia. I want to thank everyone who visited me along the way. When I look back, my favorite times were probably the times when friends and relatives came to visit me. I have had so many of my childhood friends following me and encouraging me! I believe we share a special bond of lifetime friendship, so thank you so much. I want to give a huge thank you to my Medium Rare business partners Mark and Steve, our GMs Alex, Chris, Vanessa, and Paulos, and all of our awesome staff for holding down the fort in my absence. I am confident that the Medium Rare dining experience while I was gone was as memorable as before I left. A special thanks to Angela, who helped me oversee all the financials while I have been gone. She has been mailing packages of checks to little post offices for me to sign, and reviewing everything for me so I can quickly review and approve when I had Internet access. I want to thank my current and former YPO forum members and all the other YPOers who followed this hike. Finally, all the other groups of my friends to include The BUDS, BAC United, YEO, Starlight Children's Foundation, Cuisine Solutions, CRC, 3GI, CCF, DC Running Coach, my neighbors, and other good (non-affiliated) friends of my wife and me—thank you for your support and following my hike. For all those I met along the way, or who came to my site through Medium Rare or some other way, thank you for following my hike.

    I will have time now to think about what I learned or got out of thru-hiking the Appalachian Trail. The one thing that struck me last week when Mick and I were talking to a former thru-hiker was that she said that people hike their fears. She was referring to the weight of their backpacks. Many people start with packs that weigh fifty-plus pounds, and if they make it to the end, the packs may weigh less than twenty pounds. I thought, well I only carried a lightweight waist pack the entire way. However, the reality is that I carried a fully stocked van with another person. Plus, I had the support of all of you. Clearly, my fears weighed more than fifty pounds. Still, despite all my fears, I was able to find a way to get it done. Perhaps that is the lesson learned on my supported hike.

I did not write much about my wonderful younger daughter Caroline as she is more of a private person. However, I have been working on something special for her my entire hike. As she is a big fan of the movie *Zombieland* and the Zombieland rules, I thought I would create for her more Zombieland rules I learned while hiking the AT. So, here it is:

Dad's Zombieland additional Rules learned while hiking the Appalachian Trail — for Caroline

Rule #1: No Earphones. One earphone is half as safe (unless you are listening to Harry Potter).

Rule #2: Double Back. After a zombie or bear finishes with your slightly slower hiking partner and starts after you, double back so attention goes back to your former friend.

Rule #3: If you see a tee shirt that says, "Liberty or Death," with a picture of a machine gun or "I married my sister," walk faster.

Rule #4: Look and act normal. You will be invisible to zombies

Rule #5: Catch as many spider webs as you can with your face while hiking. Zombies don't like spider webs.

Rule #6: There is no rule number 6. (OK, that is from Monty Python.)

Rule #7: If someone says that this is the last uphill for a while, they are a zombie. Get away.

Rule #8: All boys on the trail (except your dad and close relatives) are zombies. Stay away.

Rule #9: If a tent is a rock'n, keep on walk'n.

Rule #10: Don't Kick big rocks or roots or hit your knee with your trekking pole, it alerts zombies of your presence (and really hurts).

Rule #11: Peripheral vision.

Rule #12: Always thank Trail maintenance volunteers, as they make it easier to get away from zombies.

Rule #13: Family and friends together are stronger than zombies.

Rule #14: Good memories and accomplishments can never be taken by zombies.
Rule #15: If zombies attack you, have faith and don't ever give up.

I want to conclude this journal and my hike with quotes from my two favorite movies. The first is by the old doctor in the movie *Field of Dreams* who said, "I better get on home now. Elisha will think I have a girlfriend." The second is from my favorite movie, *Forrest Gump*, when he decides to stop running and says, "I'm tired. I think I'll go home now."

Thanks Tom S. for the Dom.

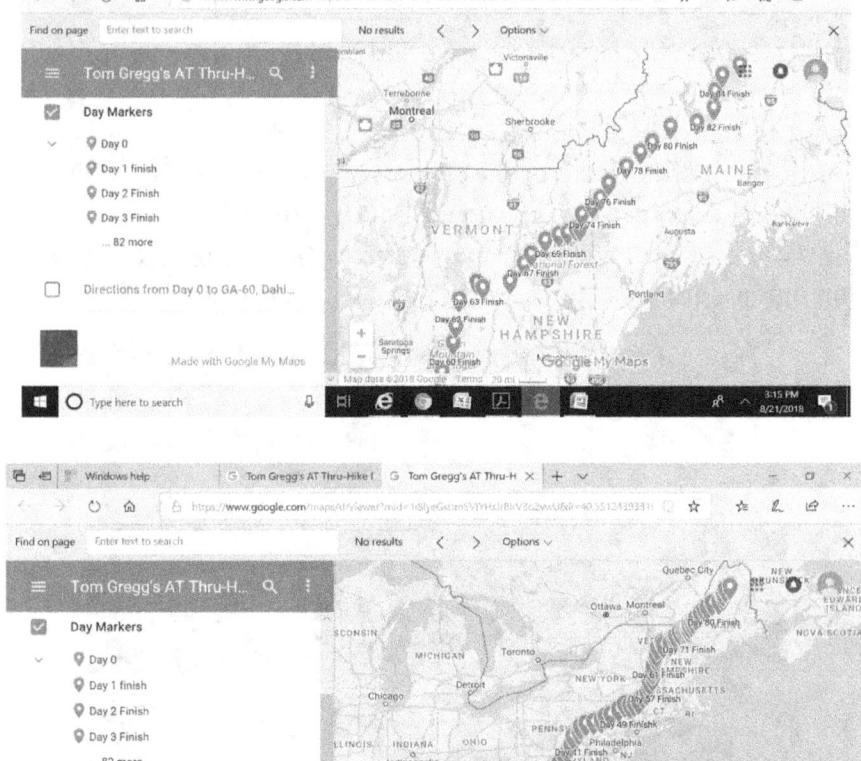

The Google map of all eighty-five days of my thru-hike.

10 Comments

Tom S.

Congrats! Congrats! Congrats! Never a doubt in my mind. Let's just hope you don't try to use this as a springboard to get on "Naked & Afraid" or "Survivor." Thanks for the daily journal entries, it really made it seem as if I was on the journey with you, but I had the easy part.

Best wishes and a safe return home for all.

Sue D

Wow! What an amazing feat, Tommy! Congratulations to you, your family and your team. Teamwork makes the dream work. Love the photo! Looks like you're on top of the world. Rest up. Can't wait to hear what's next. (Everest?!?)

Uncle Ken

Awesome adventure, Tom. Thanks for your inspirational journey and posts.

I look forward to your return trip.

Alexandra D

Bravo, Tom! Looking forward to having you back!

Marcie M

Congrats Tom!!

Kate D

Wow! WOW! What a wonderful accomplishment! Congratulations to you for your incredible journey, and thank you for sharing it with for those of us who were fortunate enough to live vicariously through your posts. Way to go, Cool Breeze <3

Steve H

When you're an (even) old(er) man, you'll always have these amazing memories to look back on with pride. This is sort of like a marathon (times eighty-five!!!) in that much of the battle is mental. Fighting the gnats, the rocks, the leg swelling, the rocks, the wet rocks, the heights, and the rocks took amazing planning, physical and mental strength, and help from friends and family. Amazing feat and one hell of a story. Great job!

Sally B

Way to go Tommy! Congratulations!!! I can't imagine hiking that many miles every day for eighty-five days! You are amazing! Eric says to treat yourself to a cheese crisp.

Rob D

Congratulations Tommy! Amazing! What an accomplishment. Twenty-six miles a day for eighty-five days. That is truly amazing!

Angela T

Don't know why my eyes started sweating when I read this post but they did (my heart is the size of the moon). Its been so much fun and inspiring to watch your journey. Congrats! You did an amazing job!

Postscript: August 2018

It is a year after my Appalachian Trail thru-hike. I think looking back on it, the hardest part of the hike was after the hike. I worked so hard for a solid year preparing for the hike physically, mentally and logistically. I worked extremely hard every day during the hike and experienced new things every day and ultimately achieved my goal of hiking the Appalachian Trail and doing it in less than 90 days. After the hike, I came home to my family and friends. That was awesome in and of it itself. I then got to tell everyone of my exciting adventure for a few weeks which I also enjoyed. Then, what. . . ?

I knew that I was going to be in trouble if I did not have new goals when I got finished. I was torn during the hike about thinking too much about "what's next" and not living in the moment. I tend to always be in planning mode for the next thing, and I did not want to do that during the hike. When it did come up in my mind while hiking, I could not think of anything I wanted to do next anyway. In the end, I had not thought of any new goals or adventures at the end of my hike or soon after.

Slowly, I began to sink into a mental slump. I still had a physical goal of running in my thirteenth consecutive Army ten-mile running race in October. It is the most important race of the year for me and all my running training during the year is to prepare for this race. I am not an elite runner, but I run pretty fast, with a goal of doing better than my time the previous year. For that to happen, I needed to start training. I was hoping that my physical conditioning from the Trail would really help me finish with a personal best. I was supposed to rest and heal from the hike. I was told by my running coach I should take at least a month off and he told me that I would not lose any of my fitness by doing that. However, after only about ten days I needed to get out and run. I quickly learned, after around twenty yards, that I would have to re-learn to run. I literally had lost all my regular running form and technique. It was a strange feeling: my mind knew what to do, but my body did not. I was used to my hiking technique, which I thought was close to my running technique, but was not. Flat-ground running had been lost to me and I would have to learn to run again. This also meant that I did not have any speed, which is important to run at the fast pace I needed for a personal best. I started working very hard on my running almost every day, trying to get to my pre-hike form.

At the same time, my feet really hurt. During the hike I would awaken around 2 a.m. every night and have to get up and rub my feet as the pain in the balls of my feet was excruciating. In the morning, I would be miraculously fine and get up and hike. Advil helped to reduce the inflammation during the night. Well, the pain in my feet continued after the hike for around six months, with it measurably decreasing with the passage of time. I had this problem after my Camino de Santiago five-hundred mile hike two years prior, but the pain lasted proportionally less time. I do not think this really affected my run training for the race, but it was not pleasant. This was the only lasting issue I had physically from the hike. I have somehow, during the last few weeks, caused the foot issue to re-appear or flare-up, but I hope it will not last too long.

The biggest general health post hike issue I had was my weight. I am normally between 150 and 155 pounds. I get a little heavier between Thanksgiving and the New Year, and then I go into lose-weight mode on January 2. Although I was now off the Trail, my metabolism was used to me hiking for 10 or 11 hours a day and to me eating whatever and as much as I wanted every day. Although I drastically reduced my calorie intake after finishing the hike, I believe that my body decided that whatever it took in, it needed to store (as fat). So, I started gaining weight. I have learned over the years that each pound of fat is worth 2 seconds a mile. I did not want to focus on weight when I returned, as I had to gain some weight back in the beginning, so I decided I would not look at the scale for a while.

My running coach gave me many warnings not to expect to do very well in the Army Ten-Miler, but I took that as a challenge. He said, you just walked more than 2,000 miles—that is enough for one year. When race day came at the beginning of October, the weather prediction was mid-70s at the start with 100 percent humidity. I knew that was less than ideal, but I was up for the challenge. The pomp and ceremony at the beginning of the Army Ten-Miler is awesome, and I am always so excited when the race begins. I usually get to start near the front, so I get to see all of it. There were 30,000 registered runners for the race, and I had my first racing bib with a number less than 1,000 (expected finish place). So, other runners see it and might say to themselves, "wow, this guy is probably really fast." As much as I wanted to be fast that day and live up to my number, it was not the case. After four miles, I mentally had to change my goal to just finishing without stopping. I usually do not drink at any water stations (every two miles), but on this day, I would drink one cup of water at every station and throw two or three on my head. I finished with one of my slowest times in eight years. They actually stopped the race for slower racers, as the heat was causing too many emergencies on the course. So, I should have been happy to have finished my thirteenth consecutive Army Ten-Miler race, but it just left me feeling mentally further down. I did not do well and it would be another year until I could try again.

Now, my one post-AT goal was over, and I really had not done well at that. So, what now? I still had work. I had three Medium Rare restaurants to run, and we were getting ready to start a fourth, but work had not yet begun on that. There were a lot of Medium Rare issues to catch-up on the first few weeks back from the Trail, but after that there was not that much new and interesting day-to-day stuff to do to keep me mentally motivated. Were the three restaurants doing great? No. Was there a lot I could do to fix them and improve them? Yes. Was I doing it? No! I just wasn't feeling any motivation to go the extra mile and innovate or lead.

I work at home a lot. So, I was feeling isolated, on top of everything else. The one organization I did not give up for the Trail was the Young Presidents Organization (YPO). I talked to my wife and YPO friends a lot about how I was feeling down with no real goals or things to look forward to. So, after the race and after talking to my wife and friends, I decided I needed to get involved again. In preparation for the Trail, I had slowly removed myself from all extracurricular activities that would hamper my focus and commitment to completing the Trail. I was on organization boards; I coached soccer; I was a country club member and played golf and tennis with people. Now, I worked alone and ran alone. I then saw my family in the evenings and they were often tired or had other things to do, or I was unmotivated to do anything.

I chose three new things to do: I would coach Special Olympics basketball; I would do running races pushing disabled people in wheelchairs for Ainsley's Angels, and I would join a CrossFit gym. This was a great decision and really helped started pulling me out my post-hike funk. Coaching Special Olympics was the best. I had neither coached basketball nor Special Olympic athletes before. I got so much out of this experience. I literally looked forward to the Saturday practice or game all week. I got so many "thanks" for doing it, but l was the one always saying thank you, as it helped me so much. It is hard to feel depressed after working with these individuals. It was such a great experience for me, and I hope I made it a good one for my athletes. I plan to keep coaching Special Olympics.

I also joined a CrossFit gym near me. This gave me a chance to work-out really hard with a group of other athletes. CrossFit is as the name sounds. You do a lot of different things to get fit including a lot of strength training, endurance training, and gymnastic type training. Much of this was outside my comfort zone. I excel at the endurance aspect, but I have no strength or mobility. My CrossFit gym does a great job of instruction to ensure I do not get injured and to make sure it is enjoyable for all levels of athletes in each discipline. You usually have to accomplish tasks in a set amount of time, which I really like. It is not a competition, but I am always trying to be the fastest (knowing that others are doing harder movements with more weight). I wasn't sure it was for me for a while, but I have grown to really enjoy it and the camaraderie. I am not at the point that I go out for beers with the folks, but I am starting to get to know some of the athletes and instructors pretty well. This has helped me a lot. I do not train only once or twice a week on anything I do, so I was doing CrossFit 3–5 times a week and running 3–5 times a week. It still was nothing like hiking twenty-six miles a day, but I was feeling like I was working hard at my fitness.

I have enjoyed the wheelchair pushing in races for Ainsley's Angels, but those races are not held that often. So, it has not been a big part of my post-hike recovery, but when I do it, I really feel good.

When we started building the Arlington location of Medium Rare during the winter, I started to get busy, which was very good for me. I had not had too much involvement in the previous restaurant build-outs, but I was very committed to making sure we stayed on budget on this one, and therefore had to be involved on a day-to-day basis. We also had some management issues with the restaurant that required us to really be on the ball, as it is difficult to staff a new restaurant when you are understaffed at the existing restaurants. There were a lot of training issues, and I like to train people.

As I mentioned earlier, I start on my diet every year on January 2. Usually within a month I start to lose the weight I gained between Halloween and New Years. I thought the weight I was gaining was probably due to increased muscle from all the CrossFit strength training I was doing. My neck size on my button-down shirts had increased so much that I could barely button my shirts. I was working out so hard—it must have been that? I felt very slow while running, but I assumed it was the increased muscle slowing me down. I decided to do a full body-fat scan that was being offered through my gym to get a better understanding. I was very surprised to learn that I was now 169 pounds and 29 percent body fat. Twenty-nine percent body fat is in the obese range. I was devastated, as I was dieting and working out hard—around ten times per week. It did not make sense. After much research on my own and talking to as many people as who would listen, I decided my metabolism was out of whack from the hike. I needed to do a reset. I could not get in to see a nutritionist for a few weeks so I decided to start a low carbohydrate regimen on my own. I had been a low carb dieter many years ago, but I gave it up because you need carbs for endurance running. I decided I would do this diet for a while and then move to a calorie based diet. The diet worked and the pounds started coming off. I stuck to the really low carb diet for a few weeks and then began to add fruits and other healthy carbs backs, but I tried not to eat breads, pastas and desserts. Within a couple months I was back to 17 percent body fat. I felt a sense of success in figuring out how my body was working and what I needed to do to solve the issue. However, it was a difficult few months feeling that I had somehow become statistically obese such a short time after walking more than 2,000 miles.

As the new restaurant got opened and we started to get past a lot of the associated start-up issues, I again started to wonder about what's next. I still had no plan. In fact, I still have no plan. I got an email from the Appalachian Trail Conservancy (ATC) asking for nominations for their slate for their Board of Directors. The ATC basically manages and oversees the entire Appalachian Trail. I decided a good way to give back and get involved was to be on the Board, so I nominated myself. Time passed and I had not heard anything. I still had a few things to look forward to for the upcoming summer. My daughter wanted to go to Norway after her high school graduation, and we have a second home near Seattle, Washington that we acquired one-and-a-half years ago that I had not spent any real time at. We did both of those things and they were great. The sun never set for seven days while in Norway—I thought that was a new and great experience. It did not rain while we were in Seattle, which was also great. Then, after I had almost forgotten about the ATC Board, I called a call from a Board member who wanted to interview me for the position. The interview went really well, and eventually I was selected as a Board Member. It was my birthday, May 20, that I realized that I had not hiked once since finishing the AT. To celebrate the Board appointment and my birthday, my daughter Sara and I went for an AT hike. It was great fun and brought back so many good memories. Just like anything, you get out of anything what you put into it. So, we will see whether or not the ATC Board becomes a big and joyous part of my life.

I was officially elected to the ATC board on August 12, 2018 which was around one year after the completion of my thru-hike. I attended meetings Friday through Sunday with all the ATC board members, people from the thirty-one Trail clubs, and people from the ATC Stewardship Council, the Next Generation Advisory Council, and the ATC staff.

It was such a great weekend. I was with a group of people all weekend who wanted to share their AT experiences, both good and bad. We all related to each other, whether a hiker, a trail maintainer, or a park ranger. I also got a text from Mick that he was spending our hiking anniversary in Germany with two guys we hiked with, Blitz and Pretty Boy. The three of them were discussing possibly hiking the Pacific Crest Trail (PCT) on the US west coast (2,600 miles) together next year.

The most exciting part of my weekend was getting to meet my hiking hero, Jennifer Pharr Davis. Jennifer wrote a book ten or twelve years back about her solo hike as a female on the Appalachian Trail called *Becoming Odyssa*. The book did very well. In 2008, she decided to try to break the woman's supported speed record for the AT, which was ninety-five days at the time. She completed it in fifty-seven days. A few years after that, she decided to break the overall supported speed record for the AT which was forty-six days, and she did it. She and her husband (support like Mick) both wrote a book about that adventure. I used her book during my hike to help me gauge how difficult a section was going to be for me. For example, if she did fifty miles, I knew I could do at least thirty. If she could only do twenty-five miles in a section, I knew it was going to be a very difficult day for me. It was in Jennifer's first book that I learned about Warren Doyle and the Appalachian Trail Institute, where I learned about doing supported hikes and what it would take to successfully thru-hike the AT. She went to the ATI before her first thru-hike and Warren (who used to hold a fastest time on the trail) helped to support her for her record.

She was completing a four-month nationwide book tour for her new book, *The Pursuit of Endurance*, when she arrived at the board conference. She was also finishing her term as an ATC board member as I was starting mine. She could not have been nicer to me and we talked together an entire lunch, which ended with her giving me a signed copy of her new book. I read the book immediately after getting home and it was a very good and insightful read for me. The first chapter was dedicated to the often misunderstood and controversial Warren Doyle from my Appalachian Trail Institute (ATI) who is right now in the process of completing his eighteenth hike of the AT. It also had a lot of wisdom and stories that helped explain to me why I wanted to do this hike the way I did. "We wonder if we're capable of more than what we're currently achieving, and the only way we can discover our potential is to test the limits, to push up and through the boundaries we set for ourselves."

I made it my plan to do things as differently as possible as Bill Bryson's *Walk in the Woods*. I meticulously planned and trained and made sure every part of the hike that I could control, I did. I was totally successful in achieving my goals. Bill Bryson struggled with everything, and almost everything he did was way out of his comfort zone and abilities. In the end, he failed to complete the Trail, but he learned a lot from struggles and failure. In the end, perhaps Bill Bryson got a lot more out of his hike than I did, and perhaps it was more positively life changing for him at the time and a year after he concluded his hike. (He definitely made millions of dollars from the sale of his book, which was far funnier and better written than this.)

So, a year later, I am on the Board of the ATC; I run and do CrossFit and feel like my body weight and health are good, and I have my big fourteenth consecutive Army Ten-Miler race approaching again in October; I have my four restaurants that I oversee with a business partner; I will be coaching Special Olympics soccer in the fall and doing some races with Ainsley's Angels. I continue with my YPO group which provides me a lot of support. I look forward to spending more summer days at our Washington state house, which is close to the entrance of the Olympic National Park (some great hikes). The biggest change will be that my second daughter will be off to college, and so my wife and I will soon be empty nesters. I still do not have any big adventures planned or "what next" solid ideas. This is somewhat troubling to me, but I feel better all around than I did last fall. Hopefully, if I say yes to enough new opportunities, what comes next will present itself to me.

My friend Gelacio, who I mentioned in my journal, and who has been struggling with cancer, is still fighting the good fight. I got to push him in a chair in the Cherry Blossom Ten-Miler in Washington DC in the spring with my Ainsley's Angels organization, which was incredible. I also got to attend his beautiful wedding in the summer. He still has an uphill battle, but he continues to fight and he has made a lot of progress.

His more than three-year battle does not compare to my three-month hike. My wife's cousin, Jack Jr., was a frequent commenter on my journal and a lover of the AT. I am sad to say that he got sick and it took him from us very quickly. Any struggles that I have had after the hike do not compare to what these families have been and are going through. I am thankful to have had this opportunity and the possibility to dream of other opportunities in the future.

Frequently Asked Questions:

I am still asked if I had any big revelations on the Trail or did I learn anything about myself that would positively change my life. I honestly cannot say that I did. I feel that I accomplished something really special, and I will always have wonderful memories and I will always be able to tell people that I hiked the entire Appalachian Trail in eighty-five days. Beyond that, I am the same person with many of the same positive traits and issues I had before I started. I believe in my own abilities. However, I still have very little patience, and I need to have goals to accomplish to be happy. I may be slightly less fearful of heights—that is a good thing.

Was the hike itself really that hard? It was. For me, the hardest section by far was New Hampshire and Maine as it was more rock scrambling than trail walking. However, I do believe that most people committed to doing a hike like mine could do it. There were no special skills or abilities needed to do the hike. I can liken it to getting up and going to work every day like you probably do now. Instead of doing what you normally do every day for eight, nine or ten hours, you walk. I did not take any hiking days off during this period, but many people have times in their lives when they have to work for three months without any time off. And, what they were doing was probably not nearly as fun and exciting as walking on mountain tops and coming face to face with the occasional bear. If someone is willing to put in the time to prepare for the hike physically, mentally, and logistically, they will likely make it to the end. There is always the chance of a freak accident while walking over five million steps. The biggest limiting factor in my opinion is weight. The less weight you carry (body and pack), the better chance you have. Many people lose body weight while they hike and shed pack weight as they become more expert, and still make it. However, many with too much weight at the beginning give up near the beginning because they think it will be too hard to make it 2,200 miles. Less weight makes a huge difference climbing a mountain. You also have to understand, just like your work, some days will be nice (like the weather) and some will not. There will be pests—just like the people at work. You just have to ignore them, put up with them, or learn to like them. Whether you attempt to do the Trail in three months or six months, it will be hard. However, pretty much anyone could do it given the desire, commitment, and time.

Would I do the AT hike again or hike another trail? Right now, no. My thinking may be very different next year or in five years. Hopefully, by then, I will have a new plan with goals I want to actively achieve.

Did your family and friends think you were going to be able to hike the entire trail? I established a very interesting dynamic by setting up the ninety days or fewer goal for myself. Although only one-quarter of the people who start the hike actually finish, my friends and family never questioned whether or not I would finish. The question only became how fast. Although my goal was ninety days or fewer, "the plan" I established with Mick was for eighty days. You can see the plan in the appendix. This gave me ten days in case I encountered problems due to weather, injury, transportation or anything else. I lost one day early in the Smokey Mountains when I did an eight-mile day that I could never make-up and another four days in NH/ME when it got really tough. I doubted my own ability to finish a few times in New Hampshire. I asked people after the hike if they ever doubted my completion and it was 100 percent "no." I feel good about that, but I think it is a lesson in changing the expectations. For example, if the stated goal is to try to get into an Ivy League college, nobody will doubt that you will go to college somewhere. My mother never understood why I would ever want to do it in the first place.

Do you now think that you could have hiked the Trail even faster? It was not a race, but I did want to really push myself and finish in less than ninety days. Deep inside, I hoped that I could do it in 80 days, but

I slowed down considerably more than expected in NH/ME because of fear. In the end, I was very happy with eighty-five days and the best that I could do given the circumstances. After reading my journal, I can see many places that I could have potentially done more or gone further on certain days. I was very afraid of the unknown. In NH/ME I was fearful of everything: my climbing abilities, the terrain, the weather, the logistics, and the slippery rocks. I was very lucky in many ways. I never had a logistics or vehicle issue. The weather was not really bad. All my injuries were manageable.

Hypothetically, if I were to did it again, knowing what I know now, and I wanted to push myself as hard as I possibly could, and I had the same set of controllable and uncontrollable circumstances, I might be able to do it as fast as seventy to seventy-five days. I think I could cut off five days down to eighty days just by sticking to my original plan. I do not think I could increase my average pace of three miles per hour, but I could hike longer every day. If I was to hike one hour more each day on average (9.5 hours), that would be twenty-nine miles a day or seventy-five days total. I think I could do this without hiking in the dark. If I was to add another thirty minutes a day to my hike or one-and-a-half hours a day more than I did before, than I would be at seventy-two days. At two hours more (or 10.5 hours or 31.25 miles average a day) I could do it in seventy days, but I think I would be pushing having to hike in the dark a lot on the longer days. I would need to do longer days in the south because in NH/ME my pace would slow down considerably because of the terrain. All the record holders on the Trail (around forty-five days) hike many hours a day in the dark. I have little experience hiking in the dark and when I had to do it on several occasions during my thru-hike; I found the footing very treacherous for me. I think I have the fitness to do the AT in seventy days, even at my age, but not the desire. So, we will never know.

Did you learn anything about hiking that you did not already know? I learned a lot. I learned to push myself harder and longer than I ever did before (eight to twelve hours a day), which I did not know if I could do. I learned to run the downhills when it was not too rocky, which I had never done. I refined my own hiking technique to prevent injury. I had never hiked on rocks liked I did in NH/ME, and learned to do them in different weather conditions. One of the big things I learned that really helped me in the north was when Elisha's Uncle Kevin hiked with me and noticed I was not utilizing the straps on my poles. I never put them around my wrists because I did not want to fall and have them get caught causing a potential broken wrist. He showed me how to use the straps to help pull me up the steep climbs. I did not accept the coaching at first, but when the hills got really hard, I understood why he taught me this. It was the most helpful hiking advice I think I received in retrospect and made the steep slopes so much for manageable.

How did you really get along with Mick? Mick is great. I could not have done this SETH without him. I worked eighty-five straight days on the Trail and so did he. It is tough spending ninety days with someone you hardly know in very close quarters with no breaks. Taking that all into consideration, I think we got along great, and when it was over, it was time to part for a while and return to my wife and family. I am not the easiest person to get along with (ask my wife and kids) as I am very disciplined, stubborn, and I really like to get my own way. I have been a CEO at work for over twenty-five years, and it is hard for me not to give orders when I am working. We kept most of our issues between us to ourselves until we got halfway, and then we decided to air them to each other so there were fewer problems going into the second half of the hike. There were some really hurt feelings on both sides for a few days, and then we were fine for the rest of the hike. I think.

Mick struggled in a few areas for a while, like ordering food to go at restaurants. Mick is from Germany and ordering food quickly when you get to the front of a line in a strange, new restaurant in Appalachia (culture) and in another language can be difficult and fraught with pressure. Once he came back with the van with nine full fried chicken dinners. There was enough coleslaw to feed an army. I told him I asked for six chicken strips. He said he wanted three strips for himself, and then he said got confused as they did not call them strips at this place and she kept asking him if he wanted dinner for which it was dinner time. Food was also difficult because he was gluten and dairy free and I wanted to eat lots of gluten and dairy—anything to add calories. After a while, he got in rhythm with finding and getting food, like I got in a rhythm hiking.

Mick and I would make a plan in the evening for the next day and confirm it every morning before I got out of the van. My one rule was that he had to be at the next meet-up location at least thirty minutes before I arrived because if I got there, and he was not there, I would not know the problem (often no cell signal) and whether or not to continue, and the next meet-up location could be twenty or thirty miles ahead. We only missed each other once during the entire hike, and that was in the first week. Often, he would drive to the next location and hike into me carrying food and drink and we would walk back out together. We would set an estimated hiking meet-up time. However, Mick is a people person. He loves talking to people. So, he could not help himself talking to every person who crossed his path while trying to get to me. He still did not want to be late, so he would often arrive covered in sweat. I would ask him why, and it was always that he got in a long conversation and ended up having to run to meet me—often three or four miles, up and down mountains, with a pack full of supplies. The funny thing is that everyone I would pass getting back to the van after Mick and I met knew who I was and was best friends with Mick.

After the hike, Mick returned to Germany and then he went to France and did some hiking on parts of the Camino de Santiago that he really liked or had not done. After that, he went back to work and has done some skiing and biking adventures. I see his life as one in which he works hard enough to afford to go on the next adventure. Not a bad life. We talk every few months, and I am happy to hear his voice.

I am often asked that if I was to do it again, would I do it the right way. What they are really asking is would I hike it as a traditional backpacker rather than a supported hiker with a van meeting me at road crossing. A year later, my answer is still the same. I did the hike exactly the way I wanted to do it and was best for me. *I hiked my own hike.*

I think more and more people will learn that *a supported hike of the AT is possible,* allowing them to hike the Trail more quickly with less wear and tear on their bodies and without having to stay in the overcrowded shelters and hitching into towns. It is very interesting that people biking across the country mostly do supported trips and very few carry their stuff on their bikes and are unsupported. Both ways are very doable and acceptable. As adventure vacations become more and more popular, it is my hope that many more people have the opportunity to experience the Appalachian Trail for a day, a week, a month or more. Perhaps as a Board Member of the ATC, I will get to find ways to promote this national treasure so more and more people can experience the way that suits them the best.

Almost everybody has a completely different experience on the Trail. By doing a supported hike, I gave up the chance to really make more lasting friendships. Some people hike with the same people they meet on the trail for six months. Others find and stay with groups for weeks and then move on to a new group. Several days were the most I would spend hiking with anyone. The backpackers also had more time to meet and get to know people at shelters or while tenting each night.

However, I avoided things like the rush to shelters during the day to find space, the partying, the snoring, the sometimes annoying people, and the weather during the night. Cell phones are great and they help a lot of hikers from loneliness because they can phone, text, or Facetime their friends and families. The negative side is that many hikers now prefer to interact with their phones in the evening rather than the other hikers. I had this experience of walking in groups and staying together at nights when I hiked the Camino de Santiago with my daughter. I really loved it, although we stayed in pilgrim hostels and not in tents.

There were many more tradeoffs for me deciding to do a supported versus an unsupported hike (financial being a big one) and how much support I wanted, but the decision to do a supported hike for the 2,200 mile AT was easy for me, and I do not regret it at all. I like to go fast and hike as long as I can. I do not like carrying a heavy pack or tent camping at night. This is me. I did not have half a year to do it, and by going fast and long, I was able to compress the hike to less than three months and still get so much joy and so many lasting memories from it. At this point in my life, I could afford the expense of having my own support van and person with me, and I was able to help run my business from the Trail. It is all about who you are and your current circumstances. Hike your own hike and you will more likely be happy and successful. I was.

Appendix

Appalachian Trail Statistics

2,189 Miles

5 million steps

465,000 feet of elevation gain

Crossing 14 states from GA to ME

Approximately 6,000 people started a thru-hike in 2017 and only 25% expected to complete

Average time to complete the Appalachian Trail: 5 ½ months

My Appalachian Trail Statistics

Completed hiking all 2,189 miles following the white blazes in 85 days

Averaged 26 miles per day or almost a marathon a day

Probably top 3 fastest thru-hikes this year

Zero days (rest days) = 0: 0 to 5 miles = 0 days; 5 to 10 = 3; 10 to 15 = 3; 15 to 20 = 3; 20 to 25 = 18; 25 to 30 = 33; 30+ = 22

Total Beers: South of Burke, VA: 0; North of Burke, VA: Countless

Average mileage for 226 miles in NH White Mountains and Southern Maine = 16 miles

Average MPH (except ME and NH): 3

Average hiking hours per day : 9 or 10

Time alone hiking: 90%

Average Showers: Around 1 every 10 days; clean clothes = everyday

Average pairs of socks worn per day: 3

Total pairs of trail runners (shoes): 5

16 bears; 1 rattlesnake; 1 moose

Gnats: millions (buzzing my ears); flies: 1 that stays with you for two miles and then repeat 1,000 times; mosquitoes: Not too bad. Oh, 1 bee sting.

Physical pain: Knee tendonitis (1 week); Shin splints (2 weeks); stomach issue (4 weeks); foot pain at night (+2 months)

Falls: 1 first 600 miles; 1 second 600 miles; 2 or 3 third 600 miles; rest of the way – lost count.

Items worn: Dry fit running shirt, shorts, socks, and hat. Also trekking poles and Osprey waist pack

Items in pack: 2 water bottles; Iphone; snacks, ID/cash/cc, TP, whistle. Optional items: rain jacket, water filter, bug net and spray; knit hat and extra layer shirt.

Number of days wearing regular pack: 3 or 4

Number of nights in Van: 75; Hotels/B&Bs: 6; NH huts: 3; home: 1

Calories per day: Unknown, but I could eat anything I wanted – a lot of ice cream, milkshakes, chocolate, chips. Etc..

Listened to all seven volumes of Harry Potter

I excelled when things were smooth and had trouble / unhappy when things were rocky.

My Supply / Packing List

I broke my packing list into several categories: Basic gear, toiletries, wallet, and office. This did not include food and drink as we got that along the way. The van definitely could hold a lot more than a backpack, but with two people, and my need to have a portable office, space was still in "relatively" short supply.

I tried to walk with as little weight as possible, which included my clothes, so I wore a technical tee (running) shirt, shorts (no underwear—more information than you needed to know), crew socks, cap, and lightweight trail running shoes. I wore mainly Merrill trail running, non-waterproof shoes. All light weight shoes work, but when you get up north, I would recommend light shoes with really good traction for slick rocks. I chose non- waterproof shoes because water is going to get in waterproof shoes and they take a long time to dry once wet inside. My shoes would be dry within an hour after getting wet. I also had the ability to change them at meet-up points with another pair. We kept a hair dryer in the car for shoe drying, but taking out the insole and putting newspaper inside them seem to work the quickest when they arrived at the van still wet.

I had my lightweight trekking poles I bought in Spain for my Camino de Santiago hike. Trekking poles are essential for the hike. I saw a few really experienced hikers not using them, but they had been doing it that way for so long that they did not want to change even though the poles would help them. I am a big believer in two poles. One pole looks cool, but you want your body in balance all the time. You do not see a professional skier using one pole coming down a hill or on a cross country course. I do not know enough about trekking pole brands to make a recommendation, but do not buy cheap ones as they will quickly break. I have had mine for more than 3,000 miles now. However, they now have a little duct tape on them and probably need to be retired.

I wore a light $8 Ironman watch with a rubber watch band. Your watch will get pretty smashed-up on the rocks, so do not wear anything nice. The rubber watch band is nice as it does not get smelly from you sweating all day.

I wore an Osprey waist pack. I really loved it. It had room for everything that I needed, and I did not have to have any weight on my shoulders. All the power in hiking comes from your hips, so carrying the weight on your hips is preferable to me than the weight being dispersed from shoulder to waist when wearing a regular pack. It had holsters on the side and came with ergonomically shaped water bottles with straps on top to hold them in that I could get out without stopping. In the front right pocket I kept my smartphone. I wanted quick access to the camera in case I saw a bear or moose. In the front left pocket I kept snacks like granola bars, along with my driver's license, credit card, and $20 cash. Sometimes I would put my head net there also. If I needed to take more food and drink, I put them in a big pouch in the back. In the back pouch I would also keep a jacket in case of rain or cold on certain times of day. This was the big decision every time I went out, as the jacket was the heaviest thing I carried and I would be a lot lighter without it. Sometimes I would only take a clear dry cleaner bag if it was really hot and rain was expected just to keep the rain off my waist pack.

I had three other packs in the van. I had a regular 48 gallon Osprey pack (the amount of volume it held inside) that I used several times in NH/ME. This is the pack I used when I hiked the Camino de Santiago and the Cotswold Way. I could have used this pack if I was doing an unsupported thru-hike, as it had enough room and good weight dispersal. The only issue was that it was very difficult to get the water bottle out and put back while hiking, and my phone was a little too big for the front pouch, making it difficult to get in and out when I need it. When I was hungry, I could simply swing the waist pack around and get my food out and eat while walking. With the backpack, I would have to stop and take it off to get food out. I would probably not choose to use this pack if I was backpacking the trail. It was lightweight, but still too heavy compared to what is out there today. I also brought an ultra-light pack (called Go-Lite) that I have had for many years. It is the same pack that Don't Mind and Don't Matter used on their thru-hike in 2004. The problem with it was there was no back support or good weight dispersal. I ended up not using it. I also had a running fuel belt that I use when training for marathons. It is super light. I thought I would use it on days with lots of meet-up points and I only needed a little water, smartphone, and ID to get me through. I ended up not using that because I became very accustomed to my Osprey waist pack and it was light enough.

When I got to the Northeast, I started carrying a Sawyer water filter. It only weighed a couple of ounces. This filter could screw onto a water bottle. You would fill the water bottle at a stream, attached the Sawyer filter, and start drinking. It helped me to have it more than a few times in NH/ME. I also carried a small plastic coaching whistle for safety, but it thankfully never came out of the pack the entire hike. The final item was TP—very important, and a small black Ziploc bag for its removal.

Everything else was superfluous (my favorite word) or just in case of the extreme conditions. I changed my socks and put hiker goo on my feet every ten miles, and I never got a blister the entire way. I never wore my sunglasses once the entire trip because of the sun. I wore them a few times to keep the gnats out of my eyes. I put on bug spray a lot in the north when I left the van. As I did not get to shower often, I did have four changes of clothes and a lot of socks (I added and replaced a lot of socks as the hike progressed). I would change my clothes at the end of the day into what I would hike in the next day. Mick got the lucky task of finding a Laundromat while I was hiking every four or five days and doing our wash.

I brought an electric razor. I decided that I did not want to look like an old man with a long beard on the trail. I look a lot younger clean shaven. However, I would probably only shave once a week. Almost all male thru-hikers grow long beards on the trail. It is a way you can recognize one another. So, I had a waist pack, no beard and running clothes. Clearly, I looked like a day hiker. Initially, when I would stop to talk to people on the trail, the conversation could go on for a while and they would finally ask me how far I was going. I would reply that I was doing the whole thing. They would look at me in disbelief. Eventually, I decided it was better to cut to the chase right at the beginning so there were no misunderstandings. I would start the conversation with "I am a thru-hiker and go by the name Cool Breeze, how about you?"

We kept all my office supplies in a big container on a table in the very back that separated the two small beds on either side of the van. We decorated the container with stickers from all the sites we passed that sold them like, the Smoky Mountain National Park and Mt. Washington. Mick would work with my bookkeeper to coordinate sending and receiving checks and other things I needed to sign. The rest I could do remotely on my laptop if I could get a cell signal. I would do my work mainly during hiking breaks during the day as I worked on my journal in the evening and then fell asleep.

I did not use everything on my packing list below, and we bought other things as we needed them, including food and drink, medical supplies, the bug net, different bug sprays, and assorted Trail magic. The folding chairs we brought came in very handy at road crossings for meeting other hikers, and I was very glad we brought them. The van that we rented came fully furnished with truly everything you can imagine, so there was a lot more stuff, but I did not have to bring it or buy it.

Basic Gear		
	9	Socks
	2	Long sleeve running shirts
	4	Running shirts
	4	Running pants
	1	Orange running jacket
	1	North Face light rain jacket
	1	Long zip-off pants
	1	Boxer underwear
	1	Waterproof mittens
	1	Running gloves
	1	Nike skull cap
	2	White and black running caps
	3	Pair trail runners
	1	Lightweight shoes for evening
	1	Water shoes

- 1 Ironman watch
- 2 Hiking poles
- 1 Osprey hip pack (2 water bottles)
- 1 48G Osprey pack
- 1 Ultra Lite pack
- 1 Running belt (2 water bottles)
- 1 Whistle
- 1 Sleeping bag (pillow in van)
- 1 Sunglasses
- 1 Roll plastic wrap
- 1 First aid kit
- 2 Chairs
- 1 iPhone
- 1 Earbuds
- 1 Phone charger
- 1 Reading glasses

Toiletries

- 3 Hikergoo
- 1 Electric razor
- 1 Body glide
- 1 Deodorant
- 1 Toothbrush
- 1 Toothpaste
- 1 Allergy medicine
- 1 Skin cream prescription
- 1 Advil
- 1 Vitamins
- 1 Shampoo

	1	Liquid soap
	1	Flying medicine
	1	Hair dryer (wet shoes)
	1	Towel
Wallet	1	Waterproof wallet
		Cash
	2	Credit cards
	1	Insurance card
	1	Driver's license
	1	ATM card
	1	Card holder
	1	Paper road maps
	1	Blue elastic band
Office	1	Laptop
	1	Printer / scanner
	200	Envelopes
	2	Rolls of stamps
	1	Ream printer paper
		Folders
	1	Stapler
	3	Pens
Other	1	Clothes net for washer / dryer
	4	Sealable containers (Container Store)
		Gu
		Gu chews

Water pills
Selfie Stick
Dark plastic bags for TO
1 Swiss Army knife
2 Headlamps

My Plan

I started creating this plan almost a year before the hike. I took all the five hundred-plus road crossings from the *AT Data Book* and put them into an Excel spreadsheet. I then created an eighty-day plan of where I could reach the van at the end of each day. The goal was ninety days or fewer, so I had some extra days for unforeseen issues built into the plan. Warren Doyle, the founder/owner of the Appalachian Trail Institute (ATI) provided me with several of his plans for varying durations that he used for the expeditions he led over the decades. This helped me a lot, as it is easy to see distances between road crossings, but difficult to know the level of difficulty each day which might affect the number of miles I could do in a given day. This supported hike was really made possible because of Warren, as there was no other resource out there for me when I planned to do this. There is a lot of experience and wisdom that one can impart when one has hiked the entire AT eighteen times. Most of his hikes were supported. I suggest anyone wanting to do a thru-hike of the AT to spend a week at his school.

You will see on the plan below that I finished five days later than I planned, or five days faster than my goal. The plan gave me and Mick all the potential meet-up points during the day. Mick and I would plan during the evening and again in the morning where we would meet each day. We printed a week of the plan and taped it to the microwave in the van with markings of how far I was going and where we were meeting in case one of us forgot. Not all the road crossing really existed, so Mick had to do research every day on the road crossings for the following day. He would use paper maps and Google Maps. The best source was the smartphone app Guthook. It would show a picture of the road crossings, how many parking spots there were and even people's review of the crossing. Guthook is a must-have to hike or support a hiker on the AT.

There are a few of the crossings that I show a date in the plan that we stayed there, but maybe the crossing did not allow for us to park and we needed to stay close by, but not at the actual crossing. The only major deviation to the plan was my use of the hut system in New Hampshire. I marked on the plan below that I met Mick and road crossings on certain days, but I was really staying in a hut on a mountain which is indicated more correctly in my journal. In Maine I once hiked down a mountain and back up the next day as there were no nearby road crossings. As the spreadsheet is so big, I did not include my notes section, which includes things like "start of bad mosquito zone next 150 miles," "start of 100-Mile Wilderness," "PA rock for next 150 miles," and "begin hardest 227 miles on the AT."

Hopefully, my plan may give you ideas of how and where you may want to day hike, section hike, or even thru-hike your own hike of the AT.

Total Miles	Est Miles per Day	Est. Day	Est Date	Act Date	Data Book Mile Mark	Road Crossing
						USFS 42
					0	SPRINGER MOUNTAIN
1					1	USFS 42
4.3					4.3	Three Forks, USFS 58
6.2					6.2	USFS 251
8.6					8.6	Hightower Gap USFS 42/69
10.5					10.5	Horse Gap
12.2					12.2	Cooper Gap USFS 42/80
17.3					17.3	Gooch Gap USFS 42
21.1	21.1	1	5/22	5/22	21.1	Suches, GA 60
31.7					31.7	Neels Gap US 19/129
37.7					37.7	Tesnatte Gap Ga 348
38.6	17.5	2	5/23		38.6	Hogpen Gap GA 348
52.9				5/23	52.9	Unicoi Gap Ga 75
55.6					55.6	Indian Grave Gap USFS 283
56.3					56.3	Tray Mountain Road USFS 79
57.3	18.7	3	5/24		57.3	Tray Gap Tray Mountain Rd USFS 79/698
69.6				5/24	69.6	Dicks Creek Gap US 76 Hiawassee GA
85.4	28.1	4	5/25		85.4	Deep Gap USFS 71
98.5				5/25	98.5	Mooney Gap USFS 83
99.8					99.8	Bearpen Trail USFS 67
106.1					106.1	Rock Gap, Standing Indian Campground
106.7					106.7	Wallace Gap, Old 64
109.8	24.4	5	5/26		109.8	Franklin NC US 64
115.7					115.7	Wayah Gap SR 1310
117.5					117.5	USFS 69
119.9					119.9	Wayah Bald
124.4				5/26	124.4	Burningtown Gap SR 1397

129.2						129.2	Tellico Gap SR 1365
137.1	27.3	6	5/27			137.1	US 19, US 74 Nantahala River Wesser, NC
138.7						138.7	Wright Gap
150.7					5/27	150.7	Stecoah Gap NC 143 (Sweetwater Creek Road)
158.3						158.3	Yellow Creek Gap SR 1242 Yellow Creek Mt Rd
164.7						164.7	NC 28 Fontana Dam, NC
166.3	29.2	7	5/28			166.3	Fontana Dam Visitor Center
166.7					5/28	166.7	S. Boundary Great Smokey Mt National Park $20
199.4	33.1	8	5/29	5/29		32.7	Clingmans Dome 6,643'
205.4						38.7	Indian Gap
207.1					5/30	40.4	Newfoundland Gap US 441 Gatlinburg, Tenn
237.9	38.5	9	5/30		5/31	71.2	Davenport Gap TN 32 NC 284 E. Park boundary
239.8						73.1	I-40
240.3						73.6	Green Corner Road
245						78.3	Snowbird Mountain 4263'
250.4						83.7	Brown Gap
253.1						86.4	Max Patch Road NC Route 1182
259.3						92.6	Lemon Gap NC, Tenn 107
267.1	29.2	10	5/31		6/1	100.4	Garenflo Gap
273.7						107	US25 &70 NC 209 Hot Springs, NC
279.6						112.9	Tanyard Gap US 25&70 NC 209
283						116.3	Hurricane Gap
288.4						121.7	Allen Gap NC 208 Tenn 70
290					6/2	123.3	Log Cabin Drive

294.6	27.5	11	6/1	no road	127.9	Camp Creek Bald side trail to Fire Tower
309.1					142.4	Devil Fork Gap NC 212
309.6					142.9	Rector Laurel Road
314					147.3	Rice Gap 9maybe no road anymore)
317.6	23	12	6/2	6/3	150.9	Sams Gap US 23, I-26
331					164.3	Spivey Gap US 19W
342.2				6/4	175.5	Nolichucky River Erwin Tenn
343.5	25.9	13	6/3		176.8	Nolichucky River Valley
350.5					183.8	Indian Grave Gap
351.6					184.9	USFS 230
353.3					186.6	Beauty Spot Gap
354.9					188.2	USFS 230
362.3					195.6	Iron Mountain Gap Tenn 107 NC 226
371.7	28.2	14	6/4	6/5	205	Hughes Gap 4040'
378.3					211.6	Carvers Gap Tenn 143 NC 261 BWRD
393.1					226.4	US 19E Roan Mountain Tenn
393.3					226.6	Bear Branch Road
396.4					229.7	Buck Mountain Road
396.7	25	15	6/5	6/6	230	Cambell Hollow Road
403.5					236.8	Walnut Mountain Road
418.2					251.5	Dennis Cove USFS 50
426.8	30.1	16	6/6	6/7	260.1	US 321 Hampton Tenn
431.2					264.5	Wilbur Dam Road
447.3					280.6	Tenn 91
453.8	27	17	6/7		287.1	Low Gap US 421 Shady Valley Tenn
457.5				6/8	290.8	McQueens Gap USFS 69
468.8					302.1	Damascus VA
469.8					1	US 58 VA 91 Virginia Creeper Trail
474.4					5.6	US 58 Straight Branch
482.4					13.6	VA 728 Creek Junction Station

483.6	29.8	18	6/8		14.8	VA 859 Grassy Ridge Road
485.9				6/9	17.1	VA 58 Summit Cut, VA
487.2					18.4	VA 601 Beach Mountain Road
490.6					21.8	Whitetop Mountain Road USFS 89
493					24.2	VA 600 Elk Garden BWRD
510	26.4	19	6/9	6/10	41.2	VA 603, Fox Creek
518.3					49.5	Dickey Gap VA 16, VA 650 Troutdale, VA
523.6					54.8	VA 672
524.5					55.7	VA 670 South Fork Holston River
528.3					59.5	VA 601 Beach Mountain Road
532.4					63.6	VA 16 Sugar Grove, VA
533.1					64.3	VA 622
536.4					67.6	USFS 86
539.5					70.7	USFS 644
541	31	20	6/10	6/11	72.2	VA 615
541.5					72.7	VA 729
543.8					75	VA 683, US 11, I-81 Atkins VA
544.8					76	VA 617
553.9					85.1	VA 610
556.4					87.6	VA 42 Ceres, VA
563.3					94.5	USFS 222
569.3	28.3	21	6/11	6/12	100.5	Walker Gap
574.1					105.3	VA 623 Garden Mountain
583					114.2	VA 615 Laurel Creek
589.9					121.1	US 21/52 Bland, VA
590.3					121.5	I-77 Crossing
590.7					121.9	VA 612 Kimberling Creek
598.7	29.4	22	6/12	6/13	129.9	VA 611
603					134.2	VA 608 Lickskillet Hollow

608.3					139.5	VA 606	
621.9					153.1	Big Horse Gap, USFS 103	
623.5	24.8	23	6/13		154.7	Sugar Run Gap Road VA 663	
634.2				6/14	165.4	VA 634	
634.6					165.8	Lane Street Pearisburg, VA	
635.2					166.4	US 460 Senator Schumate Bridge East End	
639.1					3.9	Clendennin Road VA 641	
654.4	30.9	24	6/14		19.2	VA 635 Stoney Creek Valley	
656.5					21.3	VA 635 Stoney Creek	
661.7				6/15	26.5	Salt Sulpher Turnpike VA 613	
667.6					32.4	Johns Creek Valley USFS 156	
669.6					34.4	Rocky Gap VA 601	
675					39.8	Sinking Creek Valley VA 42	
675.9					40.7	VA 630 Sinking Creek	
686.3	31.9	25	6/15	6/16	51.1	Craig Creek Valley VA 621	
693.9					58.7	Trout Creek VA 620	
701.8					66.6	VA 624 North Mountain Trail	
703.4					68.2	VA 785	
707.7	21.4	26	6/16	6/17	72.5	VA 311 Catawba VA	
727.5					92.3	US 220 Daleville, VA	
728.7					93.5	VA 779, I-81	
729					93.8	Norfolk Southern Railway US 11 Troutville, VA	
729.5				6/18	94.3	VA 652	
735.3	27.6	27	6/17		100.1	Salt Pond Road USFS 191	
741.1					105.9	Black Horse Gap Old Fincastle Road USFS 186	

741.9						106.7	Blue Ridge Parkway mile 97
743						107.8	Blue Ridge Parkway mile 95.9
743.6						108.4	Blue Ridge Parkway mile 95.3
746.7						111.5	Blue Ridge Parkway mile 92.5
747.4						112.2	Blue Ridge Parway mile 91.8
749.1						113.9	Bearwallow Gap VA BRP mile 90.9 Buchanan, VA
755.7						120.5	VA 614 Jennings Road
767.1	31.8	28	6/18	6/19		131.9	Parkers Gap Road USFS 812 BRP mile 78.4
769.4						134.2	Upper BRP crossing mile 76.3
770.7						135.5	Lower BRP Mile 74.9
774.4						139.2	Petites Gap USFS 34 BRP mile 71
784.3						149.1	US 501, VA 130 Big Island, VA
785.4						150.2	VA 812 USFS 36
795.2	28.1	29	6/19	6/20		160	BRP mile 51.7 Punchbowl Mountain Crossing
795.5						160.3	Robinson Gap Road VA 607
799.3						164.1	Pedlar River Bridge USFS 39
802.3						167.1	Peddlar Lake Road USFS 38
806.1						170.9	US 60 Buena Vista, VA
812.4						177.2	Hog Camp Gap USFS 48
814.6						179.4	Salt Log Gap North USFS 63
815.8						180.6	USFS 246
816.3						181.1	Greasy Spring road
822.4						187.2	Spy Rock Road Montebello, VA
825	29.8	30	6/20			189.8	Cash Hollow Road

825.8					190.6	Crabtree farm Road VA 826	
831.5				6/21	196.3	Tye River VA 56	
842.2					207	Reeds Gap VA 664 BRP mile 13.6	
842.7					207.5	BRP Mile 13.1	
847					211.8	BRP mile 9.6	
861.3	36.3	31	6/21	6/22	226.1	Rockfish Gap US 250 I-64 Waynesboro, VA	
861.6					0.3	Skyline Drive, mile 105.2	
865					3.7	McCormack Gap; Skyline Drive 102.1	
866.8					5.5	Beagle Gap; Skyline Drive Mile 99.5	
870					8.7	Jarmin Gap, Skyline Drive 96.9	
871.8					10.5	Skyline Drive 95.3	
873.4					12.1	Turk Gap; Skyline Drive 94.1	
875.4					14.1	Skyline Drive	
879.5					18.2	Skyline Drive	
881.3					20	Skyline Drive	
881.5					20.2	Skyline Drive	
883.6					22.3	Skyline Drive	
885.1					23.8	Skyline Drive	
886					24.7	Skyline Drive	
886.4	25.1	32	6/22		25.1	Skyline Drive	
893.6				6/23	32.3	Ivy Creek Overloook SD	
895.4					34.1	Pinefield Gap, SD	
897.3					36	Simmons Gap	
900.6					39.3	Powell Gap SD	
902.2					40.9	Smith Roach Gap SD	
905.5					44.2	SD	
906.8					45.5	Swift Run Gap US 33 SD	
915.1	28.7	33	6/23		53.8	Lewis Mountain Campground SD	
918.4					57.1	Booten Gap SD	
921.2				6/24	59.9	Milam Gap	

922.9						61.6	Big Meadows Wayside (vis Center)
923.8						62.5	Big Meadows
925.4						64.1	Fischers Gap SD
928.6						67.3	Hawksbill Gap SD
929						67.7	Side Trail to Crescent Overlook SD
931.1						69.8	Skyland Service Road (South)
931.9						70.6	Skyland Service Road(North)
933.9						72.6	Hughes Rover Gap SD
936.1						74.8	Pinnacles Picnic Ground SD
936.2						74.9	Jewell Hollow Overlook SD
941.4	26.3	34	6/24	6/25		80.1	Thorton Gap US 211 SD
944.5						83.2	SD
944.8						83.5	Beahms Gap
950						88.7	Elkwallow Gap SD
951.5						90.2	Rattlesnale Point Overlook SD
952.5						91.2	SD
952.8						91.5	SD
954						92.7	Little Hogback Overlook SD
954.6						93.3	SD
955.9						94.6	Gravel Springs Gap SD
957.5						96.2	SD
959.7						98.4	Hogwallow Gap SD
961.4					6/26	100.1	Jenkings Gap SD
963.5						102.2	Compton Gap SD
967.7						106.4	Va 602
969.1	27.7	35	6/25			107.8	US 522 Front Royal, VA
975.4						6.3	VA 638
977.3						8.2	Va 55 Linden, VA
989.1					6/27	20	Ashby Gap US 50
996.4	27.3	36	6/26			27.3	Morgans Mill Road (va 605)

1003.2					34.1	Va 7, Va 679 Bluemont Va
1016.8				6/28	47.7	Keys Gap, Wva 9
1021.4					52.3	Chestnut Hill Road (W.Va 32)
1022.1					53	US 340 Shennandoah River Bridge
1022.4					53.3	ATC Harpers Ferry W. Va
1023.0					53.9	Shennandoah Street
1026.0					56.9	Keep Tryst Road
1026.4	30	37	6/27		57.3	US 340 Underpass
1033.1					64	Gathland State Park, Gapland RD Burkitsville, MD
1039.5					70.4	Reno Monument Road
1040.5					71.4	Turners Gap US Alt 40 Boonsboro, MD
1041.9					72.8	Monument Road
1044.6					75.5	Boonsboro Mountain Road
1045.4				6/29	76.3	I-70 Footbridge US 40
1054.0					84.9	Wolfsville Road (MD 17) Smithsburg, MD
1055.5					86.4	Foxville Road (MD 77)
1057.3	30.9	38	6/28		88.2	Warner Gap Road
1058.1					89	Raven Rock Hollow (MD 941)
1060.9					91.8	Trail to High Rock
1063.8					94.7	Pen Mar Park Cascade, MD
1064.0					94.9	PA MD state line
1064.0					0.01	Pen Mar Road
1065.1					1.1	Buena Vista Road
1066.3					2.3	Old Pa. 16
1066.6					2.6	Pa . 16 Blue Ridge Summit, PA
1066.8					2.8	Mackie Run, Mentzer Gap Road
1071.1					7.1	Antietam Shelter, Old Forge Park
1071.5					7.5	Rattlesnake Run Road

1072.1					8.1	Old Forge Road
1076.9					12.9	Swamp Road
1077.2					13.2	Pa 233 South Mountain PA
1081.9					17.9	US 30 Caledonia State Park Fayettville, PA
1083.8				6/30	19.8	Quarry Gap Road
1086.0					22	Sandy Sod Junction
1088.6					24.6	Middle Ridge Road
1089.1	31.8	39	6/29		25.1	Ridge Raod, Means Hollow Road
1089.5					25.5	Mileburn Road
1093.2					29.2	Shippensburg Road
1097.0					33	Woodrow Road
1101.5					37.5	Pa. 233
1101.8					37.8	Pine Grove Furnace State Park
1107.6					43.6	Limkiln Road
1109.5					45.5	Pine Grove Road
1110.4					46.4	Hunters Run Road (PA 34) Gardners PA
1112.2				7/1	48.2	PA 94 Mount Holly Springs PA
1115.0	25.9	40	6/30		51	Whiskey Spring Road
1120.7					56.7	Yellow Breeches Creek
1121.0					57	PA 174 Boiling Springs PA
1123.0					59	PA 74
1125.1					61.1	Trindle Road (PA 641)
1127.8					63.8	Pennsylvania Turnpike
1129.0					65	US 11 Carlisle PA
1129.9					65.9	I-81 Crossing
1131.3					67.3	Conodoguinet Creek, Scott Farm Trail Work Ctr
1133.3					69.3	PA 944 Donnellytown PA
1137.6				7/2	73.6	Pa 850
1146.2	31.2	41	7/1		82.2	US 11 & 15, Pa 274
1146.7					82.7	Ducannon PA

1147.9					83.9	Juniata River, Pa 849	
1147.9					83.9	Clark's Ferry Bridge (West end)	
1148.5					84.5	US 22 & 322, Norfolk Southern Railway	
1154.8					90.8	Pa 225	
1164.3				7/3	100.3	Pa 325, Clarks Valley	
1180.3	34.1	42	7/2		116.3	Pa 443, Green Point, Pa	
1181.7					117.7	Swarta Gap, Pa 72	
1182.1					118.1	I-81	
1191.2					127.2	Pa 645	
1193.1				7/4	129.1	Pa 501 Pine Grove, Pa	
1202.4					138.4	Pa 183, Rentschler Marker	
1210.1	29.8	43	7/3		146.1	Shartlesville Cross Mt Road, Shartlesville, PA	
1216.8					152.8	Port Clinton, Pa	
1217.5				7/5	153.5	Pa 61	
1232.0					168	Hawk Mountain Road	
1241.3	31.2	44	7/4		177.3	Fort Franklin Road	
1243.5					179.5	Pa 309 Blue Mountain Summit	
1248.4				7/6	184.4	Bake Oven Knobb Road	
1251.8					187.8	Ashfield Road, Ashfield Pa	
1256.8					192.8	Lehigh Gap, Pa 873 Slatington, PA	
1256.9					192.9	Lehigh River Bridge Pa 873 Palmerton, PA	
1257.1					193.1	Pa 248	
1262.1					198.1	Little Gap Danielsville, Pa	
1269.4	28.1	45	7/5	7/7	205.4	Smith Gap Road	
1277.5					213.5	Pa 33 Wind Gap, PA	
1286.0					222	Fox Gap, Pa 191	
1293.0					229	Pa 611 Delaware Water Gap, Pa	
1293.2					229.2	Delaware River Bridge (W End) NJ/PA border	

1294.2					1	Delaware Water Gap Nat Rec Area Info Ctr
1294.6	25.2	46	7/6		1.4	I-80 Overpass
1303.5				7/8	10.3	Camp Road, Mohican Outdoor Center
1306.9					13.7	Millbrook-Blairstown Road
1310.8					17.6	Blue Mountain Lakes Road
1321.4	26.8	47	7/7		28.2	Culvers Gap, US 206 Branchville, NJ
1326.8					33.6	Sunrise Mountain
1327.6					34.4	Crigger Road
1330.4				7/9	37.2	Deckertown Turnpike
1335.7					42.5	NJ 23
1338.7					45.5	County 519
1341.3					48.1	Gemmer Road
1343.6					50.4	Unionville Road
1344.5					51.3	Lott Road Unionville, NY
1345.5					52.3	NJ 284
1346.0					52.8	Oil City Road
1347.0					53.8	Wallkill River
1349.3	27.9	48	7/8		56.1	Lake Wallkill Road
1352.5					59.3	County 565 Glenwood NJ
1354.0					60.8	County 517
1355.4					62.2	Canal Road
1356.3					63.1	NJ 94 Vernon NJ
1359.4					66.2	Barrett Road New Milford NJ
1360.5					67.3	Iron Mountain Road Bridge
1361.1					67.9	Wawayanda Road
1361.8				7/10	68.6	Warwick Turnpike
1363.2					70	Long House Road (Brady Road)
1371.3					78.1	NY 17A Greenwood Lake, NY
1374.9					81.7	Lakes Road
1378.4					85.2	West Mombasha Road

1380.1	30.8	49	7/9		86.9		East Mombasha Road
1381.5					88.3		Little Dam Lake
1383.3					90.1		NY 17 Arden NY
1383.7				7/11	90.5		Arden Valley Road
1388.8					95.6		Arden Valley Road
1391.0					97.8		Seven Lakes Drive
1395.1					101.9		Palisades Interstate Parkway
1398.0					104.8		Seven Lakes Drive
1400.4					107.2		Bear Mountain
1402.4					109.2		Bear Mountain Inn Bear Mountain, NY
1403.2					110		Bear Mountain Bridge Fort Montgomery, NY
1403.9					110.7		NY 9D
1405.6					112.4		South Mountain Pass (Manitou Road)
1409.0					115.8		US 9 NY 403 Peekskill, NY
1409.6	29.5	50	7/10	7/12	116.4		Old West Point Road, Graymoor Friary
1412.3					119.1		Old Albany Post Road, Chapman Road
1414.0					120.8		Canopus Hill Road
1415.0					121.8		South Highland Road
1417.7					124.5		Dennytown Road
1419.3					126.1		Sunk Mine Road
1421.4					128.2		NY 301 Canopus Lake
1426.0					132.8		Long Hill Road
1428.4					135.2		Hortontwon Road
1428.7					135.5		Tatonic State Parkway
1431.9					138.7		Hosner Mountain Road
1433.5					140.3		NY 52 Stormville, NY
1434.9					141.7		Stormville Mountain Road I-84
1438.5	28.9	51	7/11		145.3		Depot Hill Road
1440.4				7/13	147.2		Old Route 55
1440.7					147.5		NY 55 Poughquag, NY
1445.9					152.7		County 20 Pawling NY

1448.3					155.1	NY 22 Metro-North Railroad
1448.5					155.3	Hurds Corners Road
1453.6					160.4	Leather Hill Road
1454.2					161	Duell Hollow Road
1455.2					162	Hoyt Road Conn/NY line Wingdale NY
1455.9					0.7	Conn 55
1458.9					3.7	Side Trail to Bulls Bridge Road Parking area
1459.6					4.4	Schaghticoke Road
1466.7				7/14	11.5	Conn 341 Schaghticoke Road Kent Conn
1469.5	31	52	7/12		14.3	Skiff Mountain Road
1471.4					16.2	River Road
1476.1					20.9	River Road Spring
1477.8					22.6	Conn 4 Cornwall Bridge, Conn
1478.0					22.8	Old Sharon Road
1482.6					27.4	West Cornwall Road West Cornwall, Conn
1484.6					29.4	Mt Easter Road
1489.3					34.1	US 7 Conn 112
1489.9					34.7	US 7 Housatonic River
1491.9					36.7	Housatonic River Falls Village, Conn
1492.5				7/15	37.3	Housatonic River Road
1498.5	29	53	7/13		43.3	Us 44
1499.2					44	Conn 41 Salisbury, Conn
1512.2					57	Guilder Pond Picnic Area
1516.1					60.9	Jug End Road
1517.0					61.8	Mass 41 Undermountain Rd S Egremont Mass
1518.8					63.6	Sheffield-Egremont Road
1520.6					65.4	US 7 Sheffield Mass
1521.5					66.3	Housatonic River

1523.5				7/16	68.3	Home Road	
1528.1	29.6	54	7/14		72.9	Lake Buel Road	
1529.0					73.8	Mass 23 Great Barrington Mass	
1530.2					75	Blue Hill Road (Stoney Brook Road)	
1531.0					75.8	Benedict Pond	
1534.7					79.5	Beartown Mountain Road	
1537.9					82.7	Fernside Road	
1540.0					84.8	Jerusalem Road Tryingham Mass	
1541.1					85.9	Tryingham Main Road	
1543.0					87.8	Webster Road	
1545.4					90.2	Goose Pond Road	
1549.7					94.5	US 20 Lee, Mass	
1550.5				7/17	95.3	Tyne Road	
1555.1					99.9	Country Road	
1557.6	29.5	55	7/15		102.4	West Branch Road	
1559.1					103.9	Pitsfield Road (Washington Mt Road)	
1562.3					107.1	Blotz Road	
1566.0					110.8	Grange Hall Road	
1568.7					113.5	Mass 8 Mass 9 Dalton, Mass	
1569.7					114.5	Guld Road	
1577.7				7/18	122.5	Church Street, School Street	
1578.2					123	Mass 8 Cheashire, Mass	
1579.0					123.8	Outlook Avenue	
1585.4					130.2	Notch Road, Rockwell Road	
1585.9	28.3	56	7/16		130.7	Mt Greylock, Summit Road	
1589.1					133.9	Notch Road	
1591.3					136.1	Pattison Road	
1592.2					137	Mass 2 Williamstown Mass	
1599.3				7/19	3.1	Country Road	

1610.5	24.6	57	7/17		14.3	City Stream, Vt Bennington Vt
1633.1	22.6	58	7/18	7/20	36.9	Stratton - Arlington Road (Kelley Strand RD)
1645.7					49.5	Old Rootville Road, Prospect Rock
1650.6					54.4	VT 11 & 30 Manchester Center, VT
1656.1				7/21	59.9	Mad Tom Notch Peru, VT
1668.4	35.3	59	7/19		72.2	Danby-Landgrove Road (USFS 10) Danby, VT
1676.6					80.4	Sugar Hill Road
1676.7					80.5	VT 140 Wallingford, VT
1683.0					86.8	VT 103 North Clarendon, VT
1684.9				7/22	88.7	Lottery Road
1686.9					90.7	Cold River Road (Lower Road)
1688.5					92.3	Upper Cold River Road
1700.7	32.3	60	7/20		104.5	US 4 Killington, VT
1704.0					107.8	VT 100 Gillford Woods State Park
1704.7					108.5	Kent Pond
1705.9					109.7	Thundering Brook Road
1706.4					110.2	River Road
1715.4				7/23	119.2	Chateauguay Road
1724.4				7/24	128.2	VT 12 Woodstock, VT
1725.9	25.2	61	7/21		129.7	Woodstock Stage Road South Pomfret, Vt
1728.1					131.9	Ponfret - South Pomfret Road
1729.9					133.7	Cloudland Road
1733.7					137.5	Joe Ranger Road
1737.0					140.8	VT 14 West Hartford, VT
1737.6					141.4	Tigertown Road, Podunk Road
1738.4					142.2	Podunk Brook, Podunk Road
1745.3					149.1	Norwich, VT

1746.3					150.1	New Hamshire - Vermont line Conn River	
1746.8					150.6	Dartmouth College Hanover, NH	
1747.5					151.3	NH 120	
1751.3					155.1	Trescott Road	
1752.7					156.5	Etna-Hanover Road Etna, NH	
1755.2	29.3	62	7/22	7/25	159	Three Mile Road	
1761.0					164.8	Goose Pond Road	
1764.4					168.2	Dartmouth Skiway Lyme, NH	
1766.4					170.2	Lyme-Dorchester Road	
1780.4				7/26	184.2	NH 25A Wentworth, NH	
1782.0	26.8	63	7/23		185.8	Cape Moonshine Road	
1785.2					189	NH 25C Warren, NH	
1790.1				7/27	193.9	NH 25 Glencliff, NH	
1799.6	17.6	64	7/24		203.4	Kinsman Notch, NH	
1815.9	16.3	65	7/25	7/28	219.7	Franconia Notch US 3 North Woodstock, NH	
1843.6	27.7	66	7/26	7/29	247.4	Crawford Notch US 302	
1856.1				7/30	259.9	Mount Washington, NH	
1869.6	26	67	7/27	7/31, 8/1	273.4	Pinkham Notch, NH	
1890.7					294.5	US 2 Gorham, NH	
1891.0	21.4	68	7/28	8/2	294.8	Andgroscoggin River	
1921.8	30.8	69	7/29	8/3	14.6	Grafton Notch, Maine	
1932.1				8/4	24.9	Eat B Hill Road Andover, Maine	
1934.8					27.6	Surplus Road	
1939.6					32.4	SAWYER ROAD (DIRT)	
1942.2	20.4	70	7/30		35	South Arm Road, Black Brook (ford)	
1955.5				8/5	48.3	Maine 17 Oquossoc, Maine	
1968.6	26.4	71	7/31	8/6	61.4	Maine 4 Rangeley, Maine	
1969.4					62.2	OLD COUNTRY ROAD (GRAVEL)	
1983.5					76.3	BARNJAM ROAD (PRIVATE GRAVEL)	

1992.6					85.4	CARIBOU VALLEY ROAD (GRAVEL)
2000.8	32.2	72	8/1	8/7	93.6	Maine 27, Stratton, Maine
2001.6					94.4	Stratton Brook Pond Road
2017.5				8/8	110.3	East Flagstaff Road
2017.6					110.4	Bog Brook Road, Flagstaff Lake
2020.3	19.5	73	8/2		113.1	Long Falls Dam Road
2026.4					119.2	gravel Road
2027.3					120.1	gravel road
2029.6					122.4	Scott Road (gravel)
2034.5					127.3	Otter Pond Road (gravel)
2037.8				8/9	130.6	US 201 Caratunk, Maine
2041.9					134.7	GROVE ROAD (GRAVEL)
2043.1				8/9	135.9	Boise-Cascade Logging Road
2049.7	29.4	74	8/3		142.5	Moxie Pond (south end)
2057.8					150.6	gravel Road
2058.3					151.1	gravel Road
2060.6					153.4	BALD MOUNTAIN ROAD (GRAVEL)
2068.2					161	Shirley-Blanchard Road Monson, Maine
2071.3					164.1	Historic AT route (parking)
2074.5	24.8	75	8/4	8/10	167.3	Maine 15
2075.5					168.3	Old Stage road (dirt)
2078.7					171.5	North Pond Tote Road
2081.0					173.8	woods road
2081.8					174.6	gravel Road
2083.7					176.5	woods road
2088.8					181.6	Long Pond Tote Road (gravel)
2089.9					182.7	Otter Pond Parking (.8 E)
2104.4	29.9	76	8/5	8/11	197.2	Katahdin Iron Works Road

2119.2					212	West Branch Ponds Road / Long Brook Road	
2126.1				8/12	218.9	Kokadjo-B Pond Road	
2133.0	28.6	77	8/6		225.8	Jo-Mary Road	
2143.0					235.8	Logging Road / Whitehouse landing pick-up	
2148.2	15.2	78	8/7		241	Nahmakanta Lake (south end) gravel road	
2154.0					246.8	Wadleigh Pond Road	
2156.5				8/13	249.3	Logging Road	
2173.7					266.5	Golden Road (paved)	
2173.9	25.7	79	8/8		266.7	Abol Bridge W. Branch of Penobscot River	
2181.5					274.3	Daicey Pond Campground	
2183.7					276.5	Cross Tote Road	
2189.0	15.1	80	8/9	8/14	281.8	Katahdin (Baxter Peak) not a road	

Final Pictures

The VAN

Inside the Van

Rocks just suck when you're
Trying to go fast – AND NOT DIE

SERIOUSLY? The end of the AT was less than
A mile. It was worth the climb!

www.ingramcontent.com/pod-product-compliance
Lightning Source LLC
Chambersburg PA
CBHW050301010526
44108CB00040B/1963